DAVID GLADWIN

BREWIN BOOKS

First published in November 1994
by Brewin Books, Studley, Warwickshire, B80 7LG

CATCHING THE BUS

Wait for your bus at an official stop. All London Transport buses stop at those marked with a white flag but at a Request stop, marked with a red flag, a driver will stop only if he is hailed.

Remember that many stops are used by more than one service, and if you do not 'hail' the driver, he will think you are waiting for a different bus.

To 'hail', stand near the stop sign, not in the road. When you see your bus coming, face the driver and hold up your left hand.

ISBN 1 85858 015 3

Designed and typeset by Supaprint (Redditch) Ltd.,
and made and printed in Great Britain.

— Acknowledgements —

The first acknowledgements are to the contributors of articles whose writing, quality and content greatly enriches the book. So in alphabetical and numerical order thank you to:
'Adsum'; Ashley Bailey, Almex Division, Metric Group Ltd; R. Clark; 'Fleet Scribbler'; J.A. Godwin; R.W. Kidner; R.C. Ludgate; J. Reohorn; A. Simpson and '0129'.

Many of the notes in caption form would not be possible without recourse to the OS/PSV Circle Fleet Lists and other publications, together with those produced (often quite unprofitably) by independant groups. Many photographs bear no indication of copyright ownership. If any photographic acknowledgements have been omitted I apologize. However, I must particularly thank R.H.G. Simpson for continuing to produce his historical prints at a reasonable price of which around 20 appear in this book. Transport Museums are always a fertile supplier of information, albeit sometimes the staff are unaware of the importance of small scruffy items. Carlton Colville, Dudley, London, Oxford, Manchester, Witton (Birmingham) and Wythall all have collections that are easily accessible and knowledgeable people are on hand to help. Personnel from the Historic Commercial Vehicle Society; the Omnibus Society and the British Bus Preservation Group not only answered queries but often showed me other lines of study. The Editors of Bus Fayre, Buses, Classic Bus, Coach & Bus Week, Coaching Journal, Commercial Motor, Motor Transport, Vintage Roadscene and Vintage Commercial Vehicle Magazine all released copyright material for our use and helped in many other ways.

One of the very pleasant aspects of bus and coach enthusiasts is that, in general, they remain quite amateurish in their outlook - hard headed Japanese-style 'Company Men' can become quite half-soaked when elderly vehicles pass them en-route to or from a rally, and very many keen owners of superanuated buses and coaches turn out to be employed in the industry (often as drivers), enjoying real 'Busman's holidays'! I suppose, realistically, that is what makes the whole business of writing and publishing PSV books so pleasant, at one rally recently I bartered more copies of my books than I sold - who needs money in such company?

Finally, I openly admit that without my wife's assistance few, if any, of my books would have been completed anywhere near the contract date and I must confess that she might have had an easier life had she not married a transport employee-cum-writer - my shifts grow worse as years go on and our industry contracts. Conversely she would have missed the permanent smell of diesel, getting meals at 2 a.m., sleeping alone when I worked nights, the outbreaks of 'flu from getting soaked . . . just a part of the PSV Panorama!

— Contents —

— Introduction —

Which facet of the panorama of Public Service Vehicle life will appeal to an individual is unique to that person's intellect and it would be a brave writer who, on his own, claimed to cater for all tastes. That was recognised years ago when the first **Buses Annual** appeared and again in the **Vintage** series published by Marshall, Harris & Baldwin. In no way does the author or publisher of this series try to emulate the contents of either of these book-styles but instead, if anything, it has always been my brief to paint with a wider brush and go down more of the by-ways of Britain's P.S.V. roads and tracks. In some ways this can be a disadvantage insofar as I have heard both of our other books, **Coaching Cavalcade** and **Midbus**, called scrapbooks but the compliments have far outweighed odd carping remarks and to a very great degree this must be due to the erudition of our contributors. They vary in age between 25+ and 70+, between an ex-publisher and a couple of computor types via a museum curator, and include a number of serving (and surviving) PSV operators' staff.

No author would ever deny just how much factual information he or she owes to others, not necessarily writing in the same field, and to some extent the writing style of any author can be influenced as much by their school-teachers as other external sources. Then, too, like most authors who have worked in the field of transport, I have had to fill in reports explaining real or imagined sins - when trying to explain why your trolleybus tried to overtake another one tends to be rather verbose whereas proving one could not have been at a certain place at a given time the succinct notation 'Diagram 364. Depart Sunnylea 0900 etc' suffices.

So, as far as possible, no attempt has been made to 'standardise' the articles in this book and therein I hope you will agree lies a good part of their charm.

One external query was why we used the old-fashioned 'PSV' (Public Service Vehicle) in the title rather than todays PCV (Passenger Carrying Vehicle); the latter may be correct but 'service' is the beginning and end of our profession - as one operator said, "Service, Civility, Satisfaction are what matters".

I hope and believe that you will enjoy reading a busman's book: a veritable PSV Panorama.

1. **PASSENGERS MUST NOT**

a) SPEAK TO OR OTHERWISE DISTRACT THE DRIVER WITHOUT REASONABLE CAUSE, WHILST VEHICLE IS IN MOTION.

b) LEAVE LUGGAGE IN ANY GANGWAY

c) STAND FORWARD OF THE NEAREST PART OF THE DRIVERS SEAT WHILST VEHICLE IS IN MOTION.

— People Panorama —

PANORAMIC ELEGANCE 1

In 1939 when she was delivered to S.C. Wiltshire of Staple Hill, Bristol as the latest member of his Princess Mary De-Luxe Touring Coaches this Albion Valkyrie looked superb and it would be rather caddish to state that the cloth-capped driver rather let the side down. Among other touches of luxury CAD 195 is fitted with a sunshine roof and a double skinned door aperture, into which the door slid. Although the trim is fussy by 1990s standards nonetheless this vehicle is all part of a glorious panorama.

PANORAMIC ELEGANCE 2

One of the last Maudslay-badged coaches to be built OEH 750 was delivered in 1952 to a Staffordshire operator. Under the skin it was a normal front engined AEC Regal III, albeit with a 7.7 litre diesel and a genuine Maudslay gearbox. At the 1952 Commercial Motor Show (September 26) i.e. a few months after delivery of OEH 750, Maudslay showed their Regal Mk IV underfloor-engined coach with AEC 9.6 litre diesel power, the Mk. III being instantly out-of-date. Only eight Mk. IVs were to be labelled as Maudslays, the charade of independence then ending.

The body represents the transitional period between half-cab styles and the later full fronts and it is both svelte and rakish. Having their works at Merton, Surrey, Gurney Nutting used a 'LIBerty' telephone number (surely evocative of road travel then) but their composite bodywork - incorporating in the best traditions both walnut and sycamore trims - was not to be built for much longer, being too good and too expensive.

PANORAMIC ELEGANCE 3 & 4

These two photographs are almost uncannily similar. One of the problems suffered by coachbuilders was a fairly extensive interchange of personnel as, for example, a Plaxton draughtsman might have his wife wish to move to the bright lights of London instead of enjoying provincial Scarborough's charms or he might be lured away by an offer of promotion or greater pay. Another difficulty, and one that certainly plagued coach body builders was that their trade was necessarily seasonal and while this was not too vital in Scarborough or Blackpool, where summer work was always available, in London there were a dozen or more coachbuilders on the lookout for a draughtsman who could produce quality work, especially as many of these small firms had got left behind by the late 1930s, still offering and producing (in ever decreasing numbers) designs that were modern a decade before.

"Loch Sumart" was a Plaxton bodied Maudslay Marathon Mk. II and was delivered to James Cameron of the Pierhead Garage, Arrochar in Dumbartonshire during 1947. In 1948 Maudslay became a full member of the ACV, in effect a subsidiary of AEC although the Marathon continued to be produced for another three years.

By contrast ERR 992 had a full blooded AEC Regal chassis complete with AEC 7.7 diesel and matched gearbox. The basic outline of the Duple 'A' body first made its appearance in 1935 and it was to remain in build until 1950, this one being delivered to the Portland Garage, Worksop in 1948.

THE GEORGE & DRAGON

The well-known (if hackneyed) adage "every picture tells a story" is here only partially true. These two illustrations were found a few years ago in a heap of rubbish. What we do not know is where the George & Dragon is or was, but presumably the photos were thrown out on modernisation. Few, if any, of the passengers appear to be the same, and the vehicles seem to be from different owners. Above we have a Thornycroft, registered in Liverpool between 1910-1913, but probably a 'subsidy' or 'intervention' chassis; one of the approved models which were designed to a military specification, given a grant towards their cost but had to be made available if and when required for army purposes. Believed to be a J-type (of which 5,000 were built) K6535 was almost certainly a lorry of around 1912 used by the Army, 'civilianized' in 1918 and fitted with a charabanc body. The thoughtful looking driver wears a horseshoe emblem on his cap while three of his passengers are smoking cigars and most of those visible have some sort of badge in their buttonholes. The scene is c.1922.

The other photograph, of some 6/7 years later, shows a Dennis which, while retaining the soft top, has a rigid frame to roll the roof over and fixed glass, rather than floppy mica windows for inclement weather. Two headlights are now fitted to the Dennis rather than the Thornycroft's one and the evolution of the excursion coach has moved on one generation. The driver has a heart-shaped emblem in his buttonhole and a shield on his cap.

The headgear of the passengers and indeed their smartness is in startling contrast to the T-shirts and jeans worn for pub outings nowadays but, by coincidence, in 1992 one new coach carried the following notice prominently displayed:

In the event of Travel Sickness due to
ALCOHOL
A £10 per person cleaning charge is payable to the driver

As the driver, whether in 1922 or 1992, usually has to clean up perhaps there is some justification for this.

PEOPLE

An aspect of bus and coach operation all too often overlooked is the presence or otherwise of people. People can come 'en bloc' when they leave coaches at motorway service stations or at the Derby or at the scene of an accident. They can come singly and one feels almost unwillingly when you are the driver on some country bus route and by way of a change they often come singly when the coach is hired to take some felon who hasn't paid his parking fee or some similar heinous crime to the Court for trial. People smile, laugh, look blank, glare, regard the driver as a pane of glass or even offer him a 'gockle of geer' late at night. But they pay our wages!

Imperial Airways people on a 1930s Commer - or were they Commer people drafted in to make up the numbers?

People en masse off on a day out. Lupus Street Coach Station, London 1930s. (M & D and East Kent Bus Club)

And people on arrival at Bournemouth around 1928. The headgear is fascinating in its variety.

30th August 1950 and this happy party have arrived. Still some headgear and maybe the weather was none too hot. Fun though.

Banbury, 3rd August 1990. Forty years later it was dull and overcast as a Midland Red coach loads.

PEOPLE'S EXPRESSIONS

What a pretty little coach this was. Probably a F.I.A.T. She is in immaculate condition. And the party look British - they're off to a great day out.

Girls ignoring the blandishments of a bus. Leyland Titan PD2/12 built in 1952 with the finest of all Leyland-built bodies. The girls aren't bad either! Stratford-upon-Avon Blue Motors.

Concentration at Wrexham. The climb down from G & G.F. Edwards of Berwyn's Bedford YRQ seems interminable.

Concentration at Tavistock. Opening day of the new bus station, March 1958. Representatives of the town and the Western National Omnibus Company united in a good cause.

If this is what victory means, give me the war! Morose driver and subdued passengers. Note the acetylene tail-lamp - a rarity by 1925.

Girls ignoring the blandishments of yet another Leyland. How could they not travel on this 1950 built Weymann bodied PS2/1? Good chassis, excellent suspension and shapely body. Birmingham Corporation Transport.

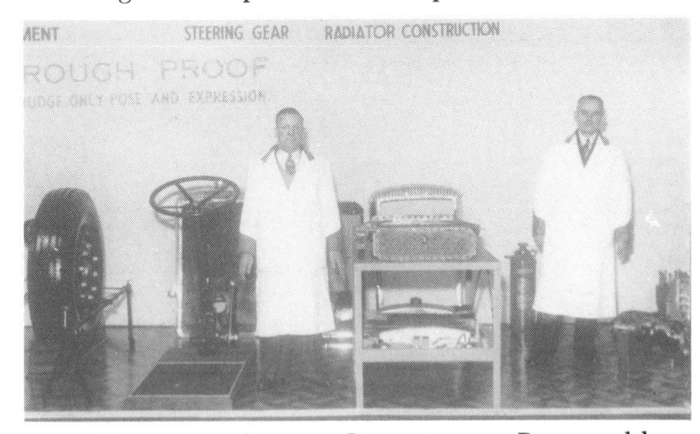

Concentration at Coventry. Presumably a CVG mock-up. The caption says it all really.

MORE PEOPLE

Photographs chosen with an eye to the combination of people and vehicles. There is a firm belief among enthusiasts that in 'The Great Days' (whenever they were) all vehicles shone with cleanliness all day, all drivers wore uniform jackets, proper shirts and immaculately tied ties. It is another belief that at the seaside you would be invited, courteously, to take a seat on an excursion and you (the passenger) would be doing the driver a favour by so doing. Undoubtedly these statements have a kernal of truth in them, but what about the drunken or argumentative passengers? And the weather? And (since they are almost human) drivers with family trouble, toothache or dyspepsia? When all or some of the minuses met, believe me the pop could fizz!

1. Char-a-bancs (or to be pedantic chars-a-banc) had their heyday from 1910 to 1914 and 1919 to 1925. Weston-super-Mare in 1921, a trip to Cheddar via Burrington Combe cost 6/- (30p) but the price of the outing to Lyme Regis is not visible.

2. Probably Hastings, still solid tyres but the advertised trip was to the Rother Valley and Sandhurst for 3/- (15p) Was the 'pattern' at the bottom of the board a seating plan?

3. People and a bus. West Bromwich bus, Daimler CVG6 delivered with Weymann body 1952. Passed to West Midlands PTE and withdrawn 1970. Bald facts, but wasn't she a cracker with bright clean paintwork. No wonder passengers queued to board her.

4. The other end of the scale, with a country bus loading. Willowbrook bodied Daimler COG5/40 new June 1938. Dual purpose bus/coach seating but by the time of this photograph she was seconded to normal service work. But Silver Service and their neighbours Hulleys provided services to parts of Derbyshire no one else would be willing to cover.

5. Although anonymous we must assume that this photograph was an 'official' one insofar as it shows the (presumably) then new 1987 West Midlands Travel livery, but look at the state of the front end! One kerb too many. DOC37V, then 1037, later 7037, was a normal 50-seat Leyland National 2, built 1980. The problem of parked cars was never made more obvious.

— Times They Are A-Changing —

RETROSPECT

by R W Kidner

Memories of buses past: so many things stand out, like my first sight of a 'General' NS while walking across London Bridge in 1923 - the low sleek line so surprising after the square box-like 'K's and 'S's. I can still picture the 'Tilling 'TTA1s and 'Timpsons' in their silver livery at Lewisham. Then when on holiday at Kessingland in Suffolk I recall wondering how the grey Daimler chara-bancs managed to extend so far beyond the rear axle without falling over backwards. Another picture: at the Doone Valley in Somerset watching holidaymakers desperate to get to their teas in Minehead climbing the iron ladder to the luggage rack of the single-deck buses, always overcrowded.

There was an early passion for London 'pirates' in their colourful liveries. I had to travel every day from 1927 from Charing Cross to Westminster, and vowed never to ride on a 'General'. There were difficult decisions; would I choose a 'Holliday & Bangs' Dennis or an 'Admiral' Straker if both drew up together? I had some rattling good trips down Whitehall in solid tyre days; we would pass the Cenotaph crabside on a wet day so steep was the camber. Unfortunately, within three years the independents were being gobbled up by 'Public' and 'Overground', and well before the London Transport Act I was having to use 'doubtful' fleets such as 'Tillings', 'British' or 'Metropolitan', unless a 'Chocolate Express' could be seen approaching.

The way 'pirates' operated was fascinating, apart from their habit of changing their routes half-way if richer pickings offered. I still have an 8d ticket issued to me for 1d on the H C Durell bus one morning, the conductor, probably a partner in the Company, confided that he had run out of penny tickets - and this was 8 a.m.! Pennies do not count for much these days, but I well remember being on a tram when the conductor told a passenger that he had over-run his fare-stage and would have to pay another half-penny. 'You'll own the tram one day son', the chap snarled.

Mr Partridge, who ran the Chocolate Express buses, used to tell how, being puzzled by a drop in takings, he took over from a certain conductor one morning. Approaching a group of men on top of one of his open Leylands, he was told 'That's OK mate, we're regulars'. It seems that some men who went all the way into London had been tipping the conductor once a week to overlook them.

The buying-up of 'pirates' was not the only game in town; there was also the great Green Line grab. I was interested in 1929 to see some new Regal coaches on the streets painted red and bearing various fleet names on the side: General, East Surrey, Autocar, National. They were running on limited stop services to the outer suburbs, a thing already offered by Premier Lines and others. This was the under-cover part; in July 1930 Frank Pick struck; Green Lines Coaches Ltd was registered, out came the dark green paint, and the gobbling-up began (Pick had taken no chances; he also registered Red Line, Blue Line and Yellow Line in case anyone else had the same idea). By early 1932 he had 226 coaches and was busy taking the vehicles and routes of 'Skylark' (High Wycombe), 'Blue Belle' (East Grinstead) and 'Safeway' (Luton). In 1933 the LPTB hardly needed its hatchet; the work had been done, and the twin disaster to the 'pirates' and the limited stop coaches took a lot of colour from the London streets.

In 1930 I was on holiday at Pwllheli, and there were never less than a dozen buses and coaches lined up outside the station, offering trips of scheduled services: Great Western Railway, LMS/ Crosville, Tocia Motors, Clynnog & Trevor, Eifl Motor Services, Aberdaran Red, and several smaller undertakings. What made it so different from today was that there were no two buses alike; even Tocia's eight Karriers were all different from each other, and there were minority makes such as Manchester, Bean, Willys, Dodge, Tilling-Stevens.

Of course number-taking was part of the fun, and nowhere better than in 'Maidstone & District' territory with some 900 numbers to find. I recall my triumph on realising that Nos. 298-313 which were always missing were in fact on the dark red Titans of the Northfleet Tramways. There were some real veterans around: No. 77 was a cathedral-like Tilling-Stevens which used to run from Dartford to Denton. One advantage of the buses of those days was that slow acceleration and the open platform made one independent of bus stops. When I lived at Sidcup, I used to jump on to the East Surrey K-type as it turned into Station Road, and jump off as it passed my house. There was a certain risk: I was once dragged on my behind 50 yards down Charing Cross Road when I got my hand on the rail but could not get my feet to catch up. There was never any danger with a Tilling; these petrol-electrics were gentle buses.

The motor-coach scene was also full of interest; roads to the Coast were full of them at week-ends, some one-bus-owned, some large fleets, like Orange Coaches of South London, who named all their fifty coaches after animals, birds or girls. My favourite was an all-weather six-wheeled Alldays & Onions, No. 14 in the fleet and named 'Sugar'. There were also some unusual Laffly six-wheelers, and some Belgian Minervas which were not very common.

The year 1930 saw perhaps the stiffest competition between chassis makers, and the greatest variety. Giving the types names was part of the sales drive. Leyland had the Lioness coach and the Lion, Tiger and Cub single-deck buses, besides the ubiquitous double-deck Titan. Maudslay offered no less than five models: Monitor, Mentor, Meteor, Majestic and Magna; Crossley the Eagle and the Hawk, Morris the Viceroy and Dictator. The little seen AJS Models were the Pilot, Admiral and Commodore, and the even less-seen Lancias the Pentirola and Omicron. TS Motors rather typically kept to numbers: TS15A, TS17A, B10B2, B10A2, though one was usually called the 'Express'. Other favoured types were the Commer Invader and the Dennis Lance and Dart (dignity and impudence). The AEC hardly needed to push their Regal and Regent, with so many hundreds of LGOC T types and STs on the order book. For bus-watching duffers it was all too easy; the name of the model was either cast into the radiator or clipped to the grill. Not like later, when to be any good you had to be able to tell a 9T9 Green Line from a 10T10.

The Commercial Motor Show of 1931 was I think the last that showed real variety (and the last with steam vehicles) and the revolutionary Gilford side-engined bus was an indicator of a different future; at the age of seventeen I became a regretful old man, bus-wise.

Petrol-electric buses operated in London for more than twenty years; this is one of the third series owned by Thomas Tilling Ltd., and has drawn away from the Pall Mall stop fast enough to require the photographer to 'pan'.

Bus scene at Dartford in 1931: Maidstone & District petrol-electric Tilling-Stevens No.75 is passing a Dennis coach of 'Grey Coaches', while behind are a Green Line 'T' and an East Surrey ADC.

The brown 'Premier' pirate buses in London were always clean, unlike some others. This Dennis (XP3760) is at Charing Cross in 1931 on route 233 to East Ham.

Buses did not come much smarter than this Commer 'Invader' (GN4793) at Dartford in 1931. The 401B route to Eynsford via Horton Kirby was a pleasant ramble along country lanes.

The end of the square-bodied era; 'East Surrey' K-types are scrapped at Dunton Green garage in the summer of 1930.

Aldershot & District were very faithful to Dennis of Guildford; the combination of double and single deck types is seen parked and driverless in the Guildford station goods siding.

Hants & Dorset No.E216 stops beside the monument on Swanage front. The Leyland 'Cub' bound for Herston Cross is notable for its side life-savers; taken in 1932.

In 1931 most of the buses on the Pwllheli-Nevin route were ex-Great Western Railway, still in chocolate-and-cream, though now operated by Western Transport. This old red Daimler brought in from 'outside' was harder to board for laden tourists than the GWR Guys and Maudslays.

In the car park at Lulworth Cove, Dorset, the photographer found a rare McCurd 'safety coach' of Enterprise Motors; the Thornycroft alongside, with its name 'Parma Violet' on the bonnet sides, is a bit old for this date, summer of 1932.

The Crosville Leyland 'Tiger' (No.347) waits at Pwllheli for holidaymakers bound for Criccieth and Portmadoc who prefer the bus to the train departing to the same places a hundred yards away.

STREETLY

by John Reohorn

The conductor squeezes between the muffled bodies that are spilling over into the gangway, wheezing from inhaling air dense with tobacco smoke. The windows are steamed up and water lies on the decking where snow has dripped from soaking boots, melted by the heat of compressed humanity alone. From the upper deck ceiling condensate is beginning to drip onto the passengers.

It is noisy. Everyone is talking for this is a works service and the passengers are all regulars, travelling together every day: familiar groups sharing the pleasures of the previous night or devising strategies to confound the designs of Management. A few solitary souls are buried in their newspapers, defying the pitching and rolling of the bus bouncing along on its lively leaf springs. The bus itself adds to the noise: the bodywork creaks as its elderly frame flexes. The half drop-light windows rattle even when they are jammed tight against the draughts, and the liquid howl of tyres surging through slush spills over the open platform and up the stairs. The throaty roar of the sturdy Gardner diesel adds its own obligato, felt as much as heard.

We turn now and run between fields lying dormant beneath the snow, waiting the imminent warmth of Spring and the quickening plough.

It is 1958 and about twelve years since this robust chassis rolled out of Guy Motors' Fallings Park factory in nearby Wolverhampton. But Walsall Corporation's No. 56 (JDH 202) is an impostor, for its body is a mature twenty one, having been salvaged from Dennis Lance No. 210 in the early fifties. These Park Royal bodies had outlived their parent chassis while the sturdy Guys had shaken their utilities apart. So thrifty Walsall united these two unlikely donors doing the transplant in Birchills workshops to produce these unlovely hybrids. The pre-war curves did not marry well with the angular Guys and the result gave the impression of a down and out shuffling round in ill fitting clothes. There were several of these unfortunates working out their existence on these second line services and by this time their shame had been compounded by the dreadful monotone blue livery with its yellow lines, a scheme that grew shabby within days. They were certainly the ugliest buses in a fleet that was rapidly becoming notorious for its diversity.

Our destination is Streetly Works, a plastics factory set upon the exposed eastern flank of Barr Beacon and decently distant from the exclusive secluded properties that made Streetly such a desirable address. Naturally a factory so placed drew its work force from more distant locations hence the extensive set of works services that arrived each morning and departed each evening.

I was not employed at the works, but at an adjacent place; the works bus was simply a convenience. In fact my home was so placed that I could and did use several scheduled services to reach my daily toil.

A West Bromwich Daimler sets me down at Kingstanding Circle and proceeds grandly towards Sutton Coldfield. Around the corner in aptly named Kingstanding Road stands another Walsall bus, untypically for this operator, a single decker. It is the first service of the day and the bus is fresh out of the depot redolent of stale tobacco mingled with the astringent vapours of a disinfectant guaranteed to purge a sewage works. Although the bus is relatively new its interior is inclined to be spartan, dolefully done out in shades of brown; Messrs Dean's seats are firmly functional. For the moment I am the only passenger, outnumbered by the crew who have slipped away on some errand of refreshment.

Shortly they return and the bus pulls away, the dependable Leyland engine lifting it willingly up the rise. Royal Tiger, an evocative name, well chosen and appropriate when dressed out in coaching rig. The workaday bus body does not do justice to this splendid chassis. Walsall had ten of them, bought in the mid fifties to replace their old Lancets. The power doors are still a novelty: just now an open platform would be more beneficial in scouring the interior of that pervasive odour. I speak of differences rather than shortcomings, for these buses compared well with the ubiquitous 'Nationals' of the present day.

There are numerous stops and the bus begins to fill with people going to jobs in Streetly Works or further on in Aldridge. The bus is destined for Bloxwich and is essentially an extension of the Bloxwich to Aldridge route making periodic incursions into the jealously guarded environs of Birmingham City, for Kingstanding was within the city boundaries and very few undertakings were then granted the privilege of plying within them. (The next decade, however, was to see a fundamental shift in policy as operators came face to face with the demands of economic survival.)

The CV6G proceeding towards the parish church is handsome with its polished radiator shell and shapely MCW body, but it is full, so I let it go. In those days West Bromwich seemed to value its image in Sutton Coldfield, and these aristocratic buses were frequently to be seen on route 51. Just behind is another bus this one running service 53. It is outwardly similar, but this is another impostor for beneath the newish body lurks a CW6G. A happier solution to the decaying utility problem. Despite the obvious similarities it is easily distinguishable from the preceding bus. It is not just the painted radiator shell, there is something subtly different about the proportions. It is pleasant enough to ride: the body is still stiff and the chassis has that cosy oily whine that distinguished the aristocratic Daimler and tamed the ruggedness of the Gardner. If the driver was adept, the pre-selector box guaranteed a very smooth ride.

The 51 and 53 share the road out past the church through Scott Arms and West Bromwich's coal mining outpost of Hampstead, but part company at Pheasey. 53 turns left off the Queslett Road and heads along the western shoulder of Barr Beacon. This is quickly turns rural making a delightful ride in any season. The Beacon itself is a public park, and alighting at the main entrance above the caravan site, I can walk through pleasant country lanes to my place of work. The bus moves on. It will cross the direct Walsall routes at Beacon Hill cross roads before slipping down into Aldridge. In my childhood I would occasionally pass through Aldridge viewing the slightly decrepit Dennis single deckers with a degree of wonderment, speculating in childhood innocence how a West Bromwich bus should appear so far from its home.

I am leaving early tonight, so no point in walking up to Streetly Works' car park, the Walsall buses will not have arrived yet, but there are other options. It is a pleasant summer afternoon and refreshing to wait a few moments at the roadside stop pole. The bus that appears from the direction of Kingstanding is painted pale green and white. It bears no maker's labelling and the usual high toned Leyland crackle is muted by the specification of its original purchaser. Any Londoner will recognise the profile at once, but should they be confused by the external paint work the untouched interior will instantly prompt the memory. Like many of its brethren this prematurely superannuated RTL is working out a new lease of life on quite different duties.

I climb aboard and the conductor leans out anxiously from the platform, taking a long look back. A figure is coming up fast, puffing against the slight grade. The conductor's face relaxes, he waits patiently. "Thought you weren't coming today". The passenger grins and dumps her basket on the side seat. "It's you that's early", she counters. A chiding dialogue develops. Although on the edge of urban sprawl this is really a country bus, the same crews running the same service day in day out. Customer care is second nature.

Harper Brothers was a large family concern based at Heath Hayes on Cannock Chase. Primarily a coaching firm they also developed a respectable network of bus services. This route ran between Cannock and Kingstanding. (It was later extended into the City centre during the sixties.) On it I can travel to Aldridge and transfer to Walsall No.6. Harpers owned several RT's all well maintained although the green livery was a little insipid; suitable for coaches but too pale for double deckers. It tended to become work-stained very quickly.

Walsall, ever watchful for good second hand bargains eventually acquired some RTL's of their own, but I don't recall one reaching Streetly; too good for works services perhaps.

Streetly had a regular public service too, the staple rolling stock being the Guys and Leylands of 1950/51 batches. These were one of the Corporation's wiser buys. The standard Park Royal body had a good clean profile and the full-fronted treatment given to the 1951 batches was very pleasing. When brand new these buses looked very smart in the lined two-toned livery with gleaming silver paint on the chassis.

This public service left Walsall by the same route as the works services, continuing down Foley Road to terminate in Streetly Village: the loading stand being beneath the trees hard by the park fence. Ostensibly for the residents wanting to reach Walsall shops, it was in the opposite direction especially useful for those who preferred the rural aspects of Sutton Park.

Another service that terminated in Streetly was the Midland Red 113 out of Birmingham via New Oscott. Thus it appeared along the A452. Its staple traffic was also shopper/commuter. The terminus was a dedicated layby at Hardwicke cross roads, very handy for the large new housing developments that sprang up around there in the fifties. This was the limit of BMMO's ventures along the A452. By 1958 this route was mainly expedited by D5's and the later D7's.

A bus can be viewed from several standpoints: mechanical, economic or aesthetic. I can appreciate all of these, but at root I tend to judge them from the passenger seat. Thus I thought the fives to be quite good being comfortable, warm and sprightly, whereas the sevens were tinny and harsh. A shame, for the Company traditionally put passenger comfort high on its list. D7's made poor comparison with Harper's RT's.

A career change took me away from Streetly soon after, but I was destined to return later. By 1968 there were major changes afoot. Many of the services were now jointly operated, especially the new ones.

Fleets had changed markedly. Walsall thankfully had lost those awful hybrids but had gained an amazingly disparate collection which was fascinating to observe but inclined to generate passenger despair or derision. Some of the mutilations inflicted on the 'plastic' Fleetlines seemed intended to re-capture the doubtful accolades earned by the transplanted Guys.

The Midland had changed too: the DL8's (Leyland PD3) always presented as interlopers despite the special front schemed out for them. The fact that Walsall had acquired some identical examples only served to emphasise their ordinariness. However the individual and beguiling D9's redressed the balance. Remarkably they were descended from the 'seven' without inheriting their ancestor's worst features. They were however too precious to be devoted to the new services that threaded the rambling housing estates. On these services, which were jointly operated with Walsall, even the D7 could be superior.

West Bromwich continued as before, weeding out their more decrepit vehicles, but remaining exclusively faithful to Daimler. The most recent CV6G's had MCW bodies of Birmingham pattern, but the newer CVG6-30's sported the more austere Orion body thus making them cousins of the unhappy D7. I will concede that Wythall's preserved 248 NEA does look very grand; time is a great healer.

Harpers gained more RTLs. They also had a Leyland PD3 with the grotesque St Helen's front, Guy's Arab V demonstrator and a brace of Fleetlines, all of which ventured boldly into Birmingham city centre to fill up in Dale End along with other routes promoted by this adventurous operator.

But decline was already in the air beneath this brave display of enterprise. Cars were on the increase and a wealthy suburb such as Streetly had more than most. It would be reasonable to expect that such an area would become a public transport desert, especially when local industry declined. Not so, services did wane and the years of P.T.E. control produced some rationalisation, but the essential pattern of services remains to this day. Indeed in some respects they seem more comprehensive. There are more operators and their buses are quite varied.

In the upheavals the Corporations were absorbed and only exist now as a token memory within West Midlands Travel Ltd. Midland Red was dissected and although the name lives on none of the three companies using it have any direct connection with the original.

Midland Red North runs services through Streetly and its recently adopted Heritage livery has brought a familiar sight back to the roads. In fact they are perpetuating the endeavours of Harper Brothers which disappeared into the National net to form Midland Red North. Nowadays Chase Buses keep the independent spirit alive, alongside Stevensons.

Amidst the trees, the grand secluded houses, the car dealers and the colourful outcrops of shops there is a rich harvest to delight the passing bus enthusiast.

C2. Metrobus D919 NDA on Service 995 in Aldridge Road, Streetly, 29.4.94 approximately 16.45 hours. This is the location of the Streetly Works Car Park, now the site of a modern pub. The trees and fence mark the boundary of the car park which had an ash surface.

C3. West Midlands Travel Ltd., heirs to Midland Red. Leyland Lynx G290 EOG waits patiently in bright sunshine, 1700 hours approximately 29.4.94. The bus is on service 118 from Streetly. It has pulled out of the terminal layby into Hardwick Road and is waiting for the traffic lights to permit access to A452.

C1. 1975 Leyland National in Chase Jaffa Cake livery negotiates the Hardwick Cross Roads en route to Sutton Coldfield. This service is one of recent origin, unknown, unthought of, in my years of association with Streetly. KNW 656N Fleet No. 34, ex West Yorkshire 1988. Photograph 29.4.94.

C4. Sutton Coldfield Parade 29.3.94. The traditional loading point for all bus services to the town. West Midlands Travel Lynx 153 is on Route 377 to Walsall via Streetly. This was formerly the joint service 77 begun as a joint service by Walsall Corporation and Midland Red in the 1960s.

C5. Another Lynx on 377 at Sutton Coldfield Parade 29.3.94. Bus 150 is in the smarter 'silver' livery of West Midlands Travel.

C6. Kingstanding 29.3.94 about 5 p.m. West Midlands Travel Metrobus loading passengers at the Kingstanding Road stop. This service is a development of Walsall Corporation Routes which began here.

Humble Duties. Arab II pauses in Bradford Place between trips to Fellows Park; the Saddlers (Walsall F.C.) playing at home. JDH 252 was new in 1944, the body came earlier! Walsall did not use a logical numbering scheme. Buses were allotted to vacant numbers which were re-used several times.

The West Bromwich fleet had a pleasing uniformity due to a prudent purchasing policy and fidelity to regular suppliers. The shapely Alexander body on this CWG 6 makes a splendid sight. The open bus windows testify to a warm day, but the dress of the pedestrians is an interesting social comment.

A truly handsome bus. This batch of Weymann bodied CVG 6's new in the fifties were the pride of the fleet for many years. Always immaculately kept, they were often rostered on the prestige routes visiting Birmingham, Dudley, and Wolverhampton as well as Sutton Coldfield.

The Grandfather. No. 2541 (HHA 1) the first production DI has been fitted with power operated doors and rear emergency exit as the prototype of a whole family of BMMO double decked buses: the D5, D7 and D9 were all lineal descendants of this bus.

Almost the swan song.

The Midland Red realm was immense with intensive coverage of six counties and six cities. The fact that it had only one route into Streetly is more indicative of that settlement's importance than company ambition. Here one of the idiosyncratic D9's threads through southern Shropshire. Several of these buses have been preserved, some in harness.

Like a tatter's pony No. 217, one of Walsall's 1951 Park Royals patiently waits its next job. This was one of the Guy buses (Arab III), efficient enough but the similar Leyland PD2's always seemed more capable masters of their task. The body has been refurbished (by MCS?) and the photograph shows how vulnerable the monotone livery was. Compare this photograph with West Brom's contemporary CVG 6. Note the paper adverts on the lower deck windows; I once had the job of printing these.

BARTON'S BUSES by 0129

Back in my youth, we knew the firm by the sobriquet 'Bartons Beastly Buses'. At the time they had a nasty habit of taking all their halfway decent vehicles off our local route, packing them off to Skeggy or somewhere similar, and leaving us with an antediluvian wreck that hissing steam and amid clankings from underneath usually found our Derbyshire hills quite insurmountable; when it still won't go up even after we had all got off and walked, one began to wonder. As it happened I worked for another coach firm of some repute and was occasionally chided by the Barton men for my comments, especially when, perhaps, I raised my voice slightly to enquire why their ancient wreck had made me late for work again. However gently I made my comment, they would remonstrate somewhat vehemently. "But", I would enquire, "if your vehicles are so good and not beastly, why is my driver (strong man though he is) sobbing in the corner of the rest-room?" They could not answer.

However, even now, feeling vaguely guilty, rather as one would after prodding a dinosaur with a shooting stick, I must confess a few of their vehicles were very appealing - when, rare event that it was, they had managed to climb a hill or two!

In the full flashy livery and chromework that was favoured by both operator and bodybuilder (Plaxtons) in 1956, URR 862 carries a light load on her AEC Reliance chassis when still almost new.

Ah. The happy days of yore when everyone from Nottingham stayed in Britain for their summer holiday, be it Butlins at Skegness, or The Elite Guest-house at Sutton-on-Sea. HVO 125, a 1947 Leyland PSI with Duple "A" body helps to shift the load.

In all her glory 462 is seen when new in 1947. Leyland PD1 chassis, Duple low-height 55 seat body.

By 1960 her body was worn out and after being picked over by mechanics for salvageable components, like dogs with an old bone, this was scrapped but the chassis was lengthened and given a new NCME 70 seat body. Re-numbered 878 cooling problems appear to have arisen.

One hopes these two were not intended to go to Bristol. 1954 Leyland PD2/12 chassis with Leyland bodywork and (after 1959) platform doors. Many Barton buses had bashed-in domes, perhaps reflecting the areas they worked through.

654 was home-built by Barton in 1951 on a Meccano-type chassis constructed from components of pre-war Leyland chassis. The underlying idea behind the bodyshell was to give customers excellent visibility and by comparison with other 1951 bodies they may be said to have succeeded.

Antiquated by anyone's standards a pair of Leyland TD5 with Roe 56 seat bodywork wait for passengers in 1953, two years after their aquisition from Leeds where they were new in 1937.

Three varying fortunes. On the left 740, a perfectly ordinary AEC Reliance with Alexander bodywork and dual purpose (bus/coach) seating. In the centre No. 940 was a second hand purchase from Crosville, Chester in 1961 when already 14 years old. 708, on the right, had a home-built Barton BTS1 chassis made from bits of two (Birkenhead and West Riding) Leyland chassis welded and bolted together. The not unattractive bodywork was also built within the Barton workshops [D.M. Stuttard]

Twelve years later, 654 was outdated and converted to a water tanker. We were told this was to run showers for cooling off overheated Barton drivers; but that story may be allegorical.

Glen was one of the independents taken over by the newly formed London Passenger Transport Board on November 1st 1933.
Recalled by Roger Kidner as having a red livery.
(J.F. Higham)

Nelson, similarly, were and independents and their three vehicles met the same fate as Glens.
(J.F. Higham)

The 'ST' class AEC Regent I of the London General Omnibus Company started to appear in 1930, in all 1137 chassis being built. There were considerable variations in body design, the LGOC Chiswick built models being of a more homogeneous style than the Thomas Tilling variant, one of which (ST 983) is seen here, shortly after the end of the World War II. One headlight is still masked and the white 'bullseye' on the back panel has not been repainted. The open staircase was fun to ride on for a youth.

STL 90, dating back to 1933 looks smart in her three toned livery. In all 2649 STL-type chassis were built, eighty (later STL 51-130) were bodied by Thomas Tilling with an enclosed staircase 56 seater design, lightyears ahead of ST 983 and her sisters. The garage plates indicate STL 90 was working from Bromley (an ex-Tilling garage) when photographed.

This 'snap' was taken 1936-7 looking to the Bank of England and the Royal Exchange buildings.
Visible with their backs to us are an ST and an LT with an STL to the right. Coming towards us in the middle distance is a Park Royal all metal bodied STL of 1937. These were the first metal bodies for London Transport (Chiswick preferring composite/wood framed techniques) but were short lived due to corrosion and scrapped in 1948.

The most unusual vehicle to find running in service with London Transport during 1946 must have been this 3 axle Albion PW 145 originally delivered to Young's of Paisley in 1937. The 39 seater bodywork was by the Scottish firm of Cowieson, and the chassis was fitted with a 110 bhp 6 - cylinder petrol engine, giving plenty of power although there were 'wind-up' problems with the rear axles, differentials being consumed with regularity as the second owner, Ansells Coaches of London, was to find out. In the background are more standard LT vehicles.

This gritty, grainy photograph taken on a dismal wet day somehow typifies all that went wrong with the London Transport so many staff and passengers knew. 319 was prefectly standard Birmingham Railway Carriage and Wagon Company bodied and AEC 6 Wheeled chassis of class C3, to some extent the run-down was the fault of the 1958 strike but the service cuts that Autumn and the following Spring were draconian. Trolleybuses are gone, BRCW are gone, AEC is gone. Even the RT coming up behind is seen no more.

(Peter Shoesmith)

Queue Questions

1

FREEDOM OR LICENCE?

For more than a hundred years the bus has served the Londoner and his visitors. It was contrived by Shillibeer in 1829 as a vehicle for all and has become as much an amenity as street lighting ; it is inextricably a part of the pattern of London Life.

We of London Transport inherit this tradition. We are responsible for public transport on the streets of London. But this responsibility can never be absolute because of the just and essential needs of other road users. Streets, after all, are not private property. There can be no bus system comparable to that of a railway on which all movement can be controlled. We must, however, see that public transport is run as efficiently as possible and that *the buses on which the Londoner relies go through.*

Today, traffic on the city streets is strangling itself. There is a disastrous confusion between freedom and licence—or is it between too little freedom and too many licences ? Is it freedom if private car owners convert public streets into private garages ? Half-cluttered streets are half efficient and this means bunching buses, crawling, irregularity, longer queues. The truth is that London is not having as good a bus service as it should.

London Transport will use this space from time to time not to air our grievances but to share our problem. Street congestion is an evil that affects all of us and we believe that public discussion may help to find a cure.

ISSUED BY LONDON TRANSPORT

Courtesies of the Queue

YOU OFTEN HEAR IT SAID that before the war no one had to queue for anything. Yet as long ago as 1936 London Transport was issuing an advertisement with this identical heading. In it we said : " London prefers the queue. English people generally have preferred it. The national quality of order and fairness finds public form in the queue."

Today, after years of queueing for many other things than buses, these words may sound unduly sweeping, even complacent. But we believe that most people will agree, on reflection, that the substance of them is true; that queueing is the fairest, the least dangerous and the most sensible way of waiting for a bus. Queues make it possible for over 600 buses an hour to leave Piccadilly Circus in the evening rush hour.

There cannot be enough London Transport inspectors to supervise queueing at every stop on any given day. So we must leave the forming and keeping of most queues to Londoners' sense of consideration for one another. There are, of course, some who take an unfair advantage of their fellow-citizens by "jumping" the queue—but, happily, they are a very small minority. So are the people who try to board a bus while it is moving, or standing at traffic lights. Apart from its obvious dangers, this practice is also unfair to others—unfair to the passengers queueing at the next stop, unfair to the bus crews who carry a responsibility for the safety of perhaps 60 people.

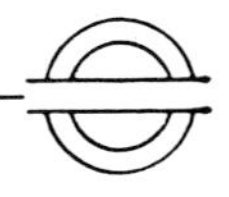

ISSUED BY THE LONDON TRANSPORT EXECUTIVE

UNEASY BEDFELLOWS

On 1 November 1969 a P.T.E. called SELNEC was formed, to take over the omnibus operations of:

Manchester Corporation Transport
Salford City Transport
Leigh Corporation Transport
Bolton Corporation Transport
Bury Corporation Transport
Ramsbottom Urban District Council Transport
Rochdale Corporation Transport
Oldham Corporation Transport
Ashton-under-Lyne Corporation Passenger Transport
Stalybridge, Hyde, Mossley & Dukinfield Transport Board
Stockport Corporation Transport

The North Western Road Car Company operations were split (much as Midland Red were to be in the West Midlands P.T.E.) and those that fell within the SELNEC area were eventually absorbed, as were the services of Wigan Corporation Transport although not until 1974.

Two buses on view in 1972, at the Market Square, Stockport. TNB 755K (ex 15) carries her SELNEC "Lazy S" and is in sunglow orange and off-white colours. Once in the Bury fleet, insofar as she was ordered by, albeit not delivered to them, she is a Daimler CRG6 LXB (i.e. Gardner engined Fleetline) with N.C.M.E. 75 seat bodywork.

The relatively lowheight North Western vehicle 2 (YJA 2) still in her 'proper' colours of red and cream has a similar chassis, but with Alexander 75 seat bodywork, although her nine years' seniority shows up rather badly by contrast with the modernity of EX 15. The North Western bus received the number 4052 in the Great Manchester PTE (successors to SELNEC) fleet, while EX 15 became 6398. [Photo - C.B. Marsh]

I REMEMBER . . .
from the Commercial Motor March 18 1955

Mr. A.F. Bird, of Bristol, now aged nearly 72, says that he distinctly remembers purchasing the first copy of the journal and has been a regular reader ever since.

He believes that he can safely claim to be the first man to drive a steam bus on a "coach" trip. It was in the summer of 1904 when a party of 20 farmers and businessmen in Shipston-on-Stour wished to join a combined railway and steamer trip from Stratford-on-Avon to Sharpness Docks, below Gloucester. It was Mr. Bird's task to take the party to the station at Stratford.

He had to be up at 3 a.m. to fire the boiler, see that there was a full tank of water and lubricate where necessary. The bus was away at 4 a.m. for the trip of about 12 miles, as the train was to start at 5.30 a.m.

The bus had to remain at the station until fairly late at night when the party returned. Some of them had not got over their sea-sickness, as they had had a rough passage down the Bristol Channel.

The interval between the two journeys was not just a question of shutting-off steam, for the fire had to be kept going and standing meant using more water. Fortunately there was a stream with clean water at the side of the road.

After supper at the "Swan's Nest", the party reached home about 4 a.m. and all the passengers voted it to have been a grand day. The station-master at Stratford remarked that this was the first combined trip that the railway had ever run. It certainly seems that it has set the example for numerous others that have followed.

Incidentally, the steamer employed was a Bristol White Funnel owned by Messrs. P. and A. Campbell, who are still operating.

Mr. Bird also remembers the reliability trials of 1907 organized by the Royal Automobile Club. These covered a route mileage of 1,000 for petrol vehicles, reduced to 600 for steamers.

He was a chargehand erector for Owen Brazil, then for Brazil, Hulborough and Straker (which later became Straker Squire) and was responsible for turning out the test wagon in proper condition. He also took this vehicle out on its first trial. The steam bus to which he referred was also a Straker, was built in Bristol, and was operated in those days by the Brailes, Shipston-on-Stour and Stratford-on-Avon Steam Omnibus Co.Ltd.

Mr. Bird started building these vehicles as wagons and buses in 1903 and later joined the bus company named. Later, the regulation putting restrictions on the tare weight reduced, the legal speed of these buses to 5 m.p.h. and put an end to their operation.

WEST RIDING DAYS

The last tram ran 'on shed' to Belle Isle Works, Wakefield, 25 July 1932 but before that from February 1922 a mixed fleet of trams and buses were operated by the Yorkshire (West Riding) Tramways Company. The majority of visible buses at Belle Isle Repair Shop, bearing the emblem of the West Riding Automobile Company (the bus operating arm of the Tramway Company) are Bristols, the maker they chose for their first 50 vehicles in two batches of 38 and 12. By 1924 the bus company boasted they had 40 services in operation, covering 200 route miles between 150 towns and villages.

RIGHT OR WRONG?

Cardiff's trams were electrified by the Corporation by 1902 and two years later had a fleet of 131 cars. Motorbuses first ran in 1907, initially to provide a service from Llandaff and Whitchurch to the boundary where they connected with the tramcars. Later Cardiff Corporation introduced six single deck buses of their own, the first running on Christmas Eve 1920.

Whatever the rights or wrongs of the underlying causes, the General Strike of 1926 had a disastrous effect on the country and some historians claim the repercussions can be felt today.

In general terms road passenger transport stopped but the strike was never 100% and volunteers quickly appeared - some daredevils, while others were ex-servicemen who saw it as their patriotic duty to provide buses to enable the innocent victims of the strike to get to and from their homes, and worked despite the appalling physical violence meted out to them. Sadly it is all irrelevant today as those who work through a strike are as likely to be treated badly by their employers as are the strikers - one thinks of the miners and railwaymen who set up independent unions . . .

Cardiff Corporation Tramways and Motor Omnibuses.

Mr. R. W. Pittard

loyally served the Citizens during the period of the

National Emergency

(May 3rd – 14th 1926) as a

Volunteer Conductor

At a Civic Reception held on Friday, the 16th July, 1926, the Volunteers were Publicly Thanked for their Services and the above-named Volunteer was presented with this Souvenir in recognition of his faithful adherence to the ideals of True Citizenship.

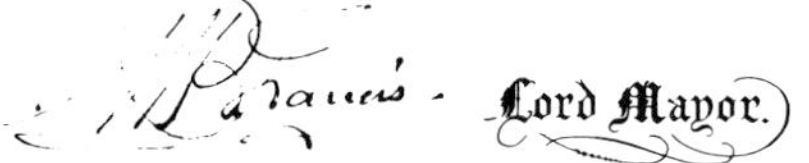

Lord Mayor.

THE RIGHT HON. THE LORD MAYOR
(Alderman W. B. Francis, J.P.)

THE LADY MAYORESS
(Miss Dorothy Francis)

ALDERMAN W. R. WILLIAMS
(Chairman of the Tramways Committee)

COUNCILLOR FREDERICK JONES, M.I.Mech.E.
(Deputy Chairman of the Tramways Committee)

MR. R. L. HORSFIELD, M.Inst.T.
(Tramways General Manager)

MR. HOWELL DAVID
(Tramways Traffic Superintendent)

AN UNUSUAL HOSPITAL SERVICE
by R.C. Ludgate

On 25 September 1972 an unusual free bus service came into being in West Belfast as the result of a contract hire agreement between Belfast Corporation Transport/Citybus and the Eastern Health and Social Services Board. An important point to note is that the service commenced during one of the worst periods of civil unrest that the city had known since the troubles first started in 1969, which involved intensive rioting and the hi-jacking of vehicles of all kinds, especially buses, which at the time was particularly prevalent in the west of the city. Basically the free bus service had been introduced for the benefit of outpatients attending the Royal Victoria Hospital, situated at the junction of the Grosvenor/Falls Roads, enabling them to travel by bus, despite the fact that at times the ordinary regular services had been suspended which happened quite frequently because of the continuing civil unrest, whilst the special bus with its distinctive markings operated unhindered, more or less, to and from the hospital. For example in August 1973, all regular bus services were withdrawn in West Belfast for a period of 5 weeks apparently because of the escalating violence and hi-jackings of vehicles. Despite this Daimler Fleetline 2558 maintained the special service, under very adverse and trying conditions, assisted at times by sister vehicle 2556; consequently they were the only bus(es) to be found operating in that part of the city, despite the troubles during that period.

The service was operated daily - Mondays to Fridays only, from Donegall Square East (later moved to Upper Queen Street) at half-hourly intervals from 07.30 till 22.00 via Howard Street and Grosvenor Road and returning at 07.45 till 22.30 via Falls Road, Divis Street and King Street. A stipulation for intending passengers required that outpatients attending the hospital had to have an appointment card, similarly hospital staff could also use the service provided they had an identity card - a hospital employee travelled on the bus at all times to check the passengers - no fares were charged.

The first vehicle allotted to this duty was Potter bodied Daimler Fleetline CRG6LX 729 (729 UZ) (which later became 2729 on the formation of Citybus in April 1973. It carried distinctive markings to differentiate it from ordinary service buses, these included large white circular panels, incorporating a red cross, which were fitted to the front, rear and sides of the bus; in addition full length narrow white panels, bearing the legend in black letters 'ROYAL VICTORIA HOSPITAL OUTPATIENTS SERVICE' were fitted on both sides below the lower saloon windows. 729/2729 operated this free bus service until the end of May 1973, when it was taken off the service and returned to normal workings. The distinctive markings were removed and transferred to its successor which was Alexander bodied Leyland Atlantean PDR/1 2551 (5540 XI) which operated the service until November 1975, when it was withdrawn due to a major mechanical fault (it was later sold to the Londonderry & Lough Swilly Rly.Co.). 2551 had been earmarked for this duty as it was the only double-decker not fitted for OMO working. Its replacement was M.H. Cars bodied Daimler Fleetline 2558 (558 E2), which had similar distinctive markings and was also the spare bus for 2551 - on occasions, which were rare indeed, 2551/2558 could be seen working the service together. 2558 continued on this duty until March 1977, when the first batch of second-hand AEC Merlins, which had been acquired from London Transport, via a dealer, arrived to fill the gaps left as a result of continuing terrorist hi-jackings of buses, in which case often they were complete write-offs. However one of the Merlins was taken from this batch, namely 2536 (AML 625 H) and allocated to this duty, after acquiring the appropriate distinctive markings from 2558 and continued on it until April 1980, when it was replaced by another Merlin, this time 2517 (VLW 364G) which was one of a number transferred from Ulsterbus to Citybus, it continued on this duty until 15 October 1980 when yet again another Merlin 2534 (WLT 619G) took over from 2517, as the latter had developed mechanical trouble. However, 2534 was only to operate on this duty for two days, as the service was suddenly withdrawn on 17 October 1980 after the last journey - the 22.30 from the hospital to the city centre. The withdrawal of this extensively used free bus service was largely due to Government cuts at that time in the Northern Ireland Health Service.

Finally great credit must go to the drivers, who maintained this special service during its 8 years of operation, often as not under the most trying and arduous conditions imaginable.

CITYBUS. A rare view taken in the summer of 1974, depicting Leyland Atlantean PDR/1/1/ Alexander 2551 (5540 XL) and Daimler Fleetline/ M.H. Cars 2558 (558 EZ) together in Donegall Square East. 2558 was taking over the duty whilst 2551 returned to the depot. [R.C. Ludgate]

BELFAST CORPORATION. Potter bodied Daimler Fleetline CRG 6LX 729 (729 UZ) seen here at Donegall Square East during the first week of operation in September 1972. [R.C. Ludgate]

CITYBUS. Ex London Transport AEC Merlin 2517 (VLW 346G) seen leaving Upper Queen Street departure point en route to the Hospital, in Ocotber 1980, during the last week of operation. [R.C. Ludgate]

IT ALMOST WORKED

'National' once meant the union of the greatest part of our bus and coach services. Towards the end, most of the problems had been eradicated with the livery blandness, green, red or white, being replaced by more individual treatments, National Express was making the railway operators look to their laurels, and the internecine battles within the Company had died away. Additionally they had gone from a loss making group to a profitable concern, albeit with declining profits.

These illustrations are merely intended to give some idea of the scope of the company; but the sheer variety of items involved was awesome.

And both the colours and Fiery Fred were alive in 1992

National Welsh (South Wales Transport) advertising National holidays.

And bus stops

ENQUIRIES CARDIFF (0222)371331

Days of operation.
These appear at the head of each column

D	Daily	F	Fridays (only)
M	Mondays (only)	S	Saturdays (only)
T	Tuesdays (only)	Su	Sundays (only)
W	Wednesdays (only)	N	Not
Th	Thursdays (only)		

The following codes and symbols have a standard application throughout the Guide

- **C** Change Coaches
- **R** Refreshment stop
- Connection in adjacent column(s)
- Connection with Shipping Services
- Connection with Air Services
- Connection with Hovercraft
- Swan National car rental facilities available
- S, DR & PR – Single, Day Return & Period Return Fares

For special Summaries of Connections at Cheltenham see Table No. 458 Composite timetables appear at the beginning of the North East, Midlands and North West area sections.

Bookmark/calendar

NATIONAL TRAVEL (NORTH WEST) LTD

NATIONAL EXPRESS

National Express is our day-to-day, place to place service. It covers thousands of towns and cities and suburbs and harbours and resorts and villages all up and down England, Scotland and Wales

It's a most economical way to travel from one place to another, and it offers a comfortable seat through the countryside in between.

Join our National savings movement — your money goes miles further on National Express.

Book where you see this sign

NATIONAL CHARTER

We have coaches throughout the area ready for one-way or round trip charter assignments.

They have different seating capacities, strategically located garages and service centres, courteous and efficient drivers.

National Travel charter packages can include suggested itineraries, sightseeing arrangements, accommodation, meals, theatre and concert tickets, conference facilities — in fact anything a group like yours might need.

So for coach charter in Britain or to the Continent, for school outings or a day in the country, for a trip to the coast or a night at the Theatre give us a ring and talk over your requirements with the experts.

Quotations a pleasure.
Telephone:
061-236 8122 or
Blackpool (0253) 20051

Bookmark

Slogan famous throughout the National Express fleet. Sometimes they mean it!

National (Royal Blue) preserved in coach livery.

And garages (Digbeth)

LONDON EXPRESS

National National

Says it all really, 15 March 1975

It's there somewhere . . . under the Leyland badge.

Good advertisement for an excellent service.

THE WAR AND ITS AFTERMATH

The use of producer gas to drive PSVs in Britain was neither popular nor successful, but maybe the first led to the second as in Germany wood, anthracite, fish oil, lignite and sugar by-products were all tried and in general their bus services ran reasonably well, until bombing caused total chaos.

The heating of Welsh anthracite 'beans' with water provided a fairly volatile gas and from one filling, with care, a driver could expect to obtain 80 miles (129 km) of travel. In February 1940, John Heaton the Chairman of Thomas Tilling announced that at Bristol there were sufficient components in hand to manufacture 600 self-contained mobile units: experiments with 'built-in' burners were unsuccessful, leaks kippering passengers! Eastern National obtained a number of sets but sensibly converted the fleet at just one depot, Malden, where bunkering and cleaning facilities were installed, and the use of spare trailers with quick release fittings enabled a bus to drop its burner, collect a new one and be on its way in 10-15 minutes.

The Ministry of War Transport told 57 large provincial operators to convert 10% of their fleets to gas propulsion but probably no more than ½% of all vehicles were so treated. There were problems (although many could have been solved with a little enthusiasm), companies claiming that engine wear was abnormally high, pistons and liners requiring renewal every two months, and that the trailers would 'shake the fire out'.

One problem was that the fire needed a good draught to produce an adequate supply of gas but as this declined so did the speed of the bus, the fire then choking. Conversely Eastern National by 1942 claimed to have run 2,500,000 miles (4.023m km) on gas, saving 415,000 gallons of imported oil - oil brought by the U-boats favourite targets, tankers. In 1942 ReDeX brought out a special lubricator to suit producer gas engines "With the Lubrocharger fitted (on the producer side of the gas butterfly) the Redex mist mixes with the gas and deposits a strengthened oil film on the valves and cylinders from the moment that the engine starts. It likewise coats the dust and carbon particles and makes them non-abrasive. Gums and carbons are dispersed and inhibited by the carbon repellent constituents. The gas butterfly is kept clean and lubricated, and frequent cleaning of the manifold is avoided. The dry-burning tendencies of gas on valves is corrected, also the corrosion caused by moisture picked up in the water washing or by water injection on the fire bed, and by gas contaminents of the ammonia type. The improvement in performance is immediately evident. Hill climbing is one gear better, and maximum speed is increased by about 6 miles per hour. Starting, idling, acceleration and pulling are all noticeably better. These results have been confirmed by some of the leading manufacturers of producer gas plant . . .", but this was too late for the companies who had turned their faces against 'artificial' fuels. East Kent were slow to carry out any conversions and then only modifying a total of five double-deckers to run on gas during 1943 and 1944. The photographs A + B show one of them, a Leyland Titan, with its unit in place and the detail of the 'gubbins' itself. (Both photographs courtesy of M & D and East Kent Bus Club).

▲
A

B
▼

A London Transport trolleybus with all the paraphernalia of war visible, anti-blast netting at the windows, white paint but (and its important) the headlights are not masked. Abbey Wood is the location.

[W.J. Haynes]

A Dodge coach with Duple bodywork typical of postwar years is seen in 1940. This has masked headlights but no white-lining to the wings. Destination appears to be Sevenoaks, the London Transport STL passing has her white marker or bullseye visible on the back panel.

[M & D and East Kent Bus Club]

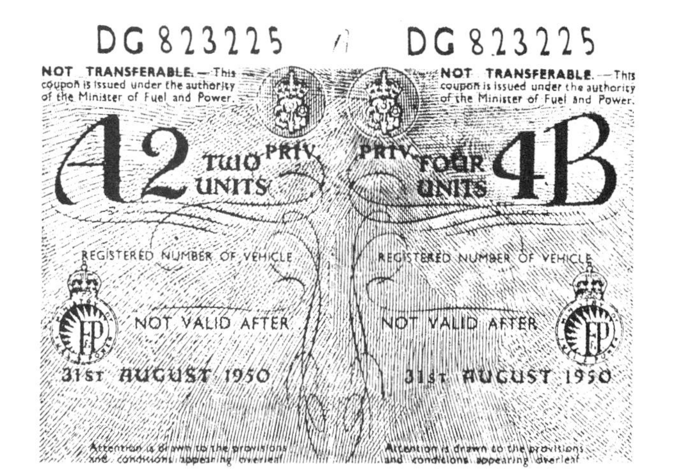

DG 823225 | DG 823225

NOT TRANSFERABLE.—This coupon is issued under the authority of the Minister of Fuel and Power. | NOT TRANSFERABLE.—This coupon is issued under the authority of the Minister of Fuel and Power.

A2 TWO PRIV. UNITS | PRIV. FOUR UNITS 4B

REGISTERED NUMBER OF VEHICLE | REGISTERED NUMBER OF VEHICLE

NOT VALID AFTER 31st AUGUST 1950 | NOT VALID AFTER 31st AUGUST 1950

Attention is drawn to the provisions and conditions appearing overleaf. | Attention is drawn to the provisions and conditions appearing overleaf.

Postwar issue by the Ministry of Fuel & Power to Govermnment employee. A rare survivor. A 'unit' was the quantity allowed at the time according to the stocks available. Normally a gallon, but could be as low as a quart (roughly a litre).

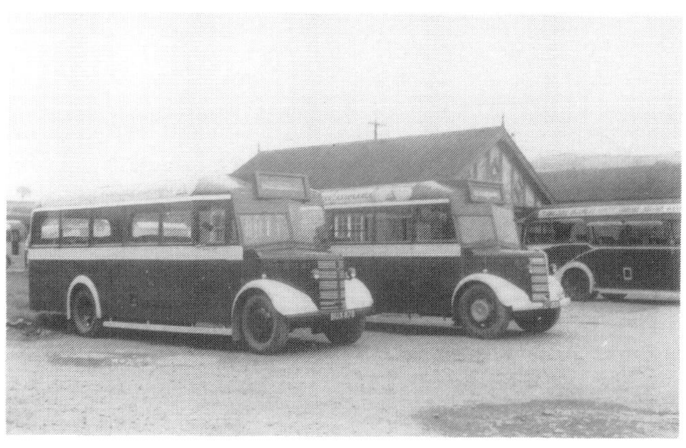

Wartime 'Utility' Bedford OWB buses - the only class of single deckers allowed to be built. These were in the fleet of Mid-Wales Motorways in 1951; the author's main regret in life is that he has never been able to obtain one since.

Advertising during wartime and after continued although restricted not only by the non-availability of the machines or their components but also as paper shortages led to the space allocated to advertisement being restricted by Government decree. Censorship also played a part, here an AEC display has been 'nobbled' by the figure of a nurse on the left, reminding one of rubber shortages with her 'nurse those tyres'. Issued 1943.

NOBEL CHEMICAL FINISHES LIMITED
SLOUGH (Associated with Imperial Chemical Industries Limited) BUCKS

OWING TO WAR RESTRICTIONS
WE ***CANNOT*** SUPPLY ALL WE USED TO SUPPLY
BUT WE ***WILL*** SUPPLY ALL WE ***CAN*** SUPPLY

SEND YOUR PROBLEMS
TO
KEARSLEY'S
VARNISH & PAINT WORKS
RIPON
1837–1943

▲ The bold (albeit dog-less) Dulux advertisement of 1935 contrasts with that of Kearsleys which appeared in November 1943.

By 1946 some manufacturers left with enormous factories which had only produced one specialized product were thrashing around for other outlets. Rather a sad decline from the essential 'Mosquito' to trying to provide bits of buses. ►

Two from 1948. Curious contradiction unless Roe had an eye on the export market.

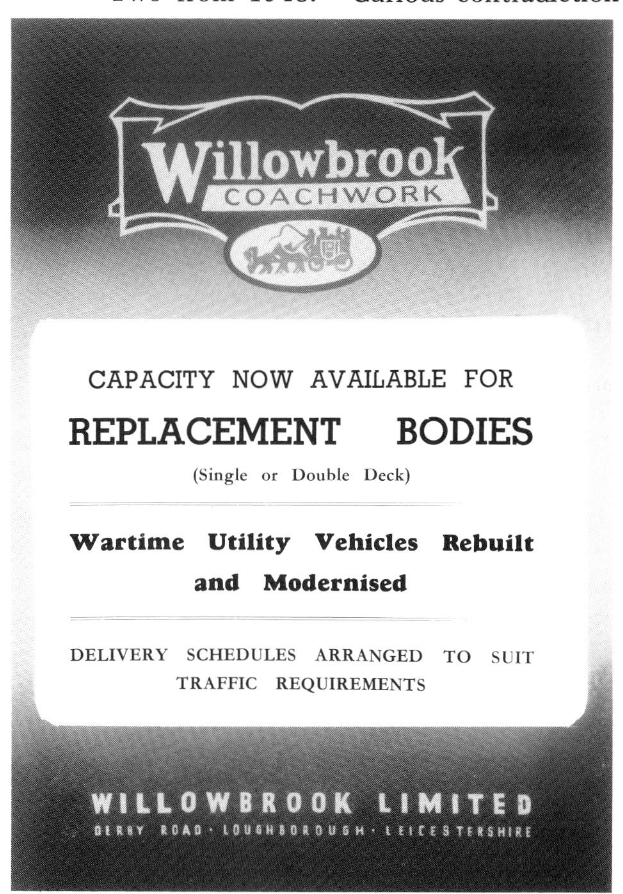

By 1951 many wartime bodies built of green (unseasoned) wood by unskilled labour were rotten. Willowbrook offered their services.

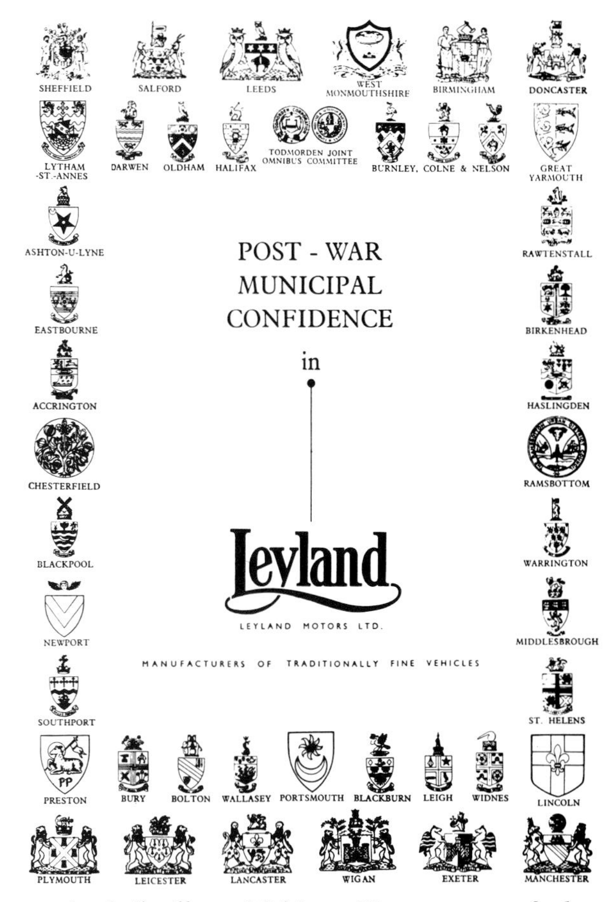

And finally - 1946. How many of these municipalities are left? And how few bus fleets.

SEE THE WORLD BY LODEKKA

The Remarkable Story of Top Deck Travel

by John A. Godwin

As part of the British Transport Commission, Bristol Commercial Vehicles developed a new double-deck vehicle for the state-owned bus sector in the late 1950s. The Lodekka, as it was named, was a replacement product for the ageing Bristol K-series, and this most popular and reliable of public service vehicles became a common sight throughout England, Wales and Scotland during the 1960s. The average Lodekka, however, had a short life, and most of those surviving beyond their 21st birthday were confined to an arduous career as driver training vehicles. Changing legislation has ended this lease of life, and aside from a very few examples now preserved by caring owners, nearly all of this famous breed have passed via the scrap-men at Barnsley to the great terminus in the sky.

Of course, there has to be an exception. For over twenty years, a London based company has been using the remarkable reliability and rugged construction of the Bristol Lodekka and its Eastern Coach Works bodywork for an alternative operation. If during your holidays in Seville or The Sahara you witnessed an orange and cream Lodekka with a number plate that rightfully belongs to the Isle of Wight, then you will probably already know a little about globe-trotting Lodekkas . . . . . for this is the remarkable world of Top Deck Travel.

Established in the early 1970s, Argas Persicus Limited of London (a company owned and operated by Australians and New Zealanders) acquired a pair of Bristol K5Gs from the Yorkshire area. These 1954 vehicles were extensively converted to create a "Deckerhome" format, for comprehensive tours throughout mainland Europe. The experimental duo were so successful at operating this new type of holiday experience, that they were soon joined by a number of Bristol Lodekkas: early examples of the rear entrance LD-type were becoming available from certain National Bus Company subsidiary companies, particularly Southern Vectis and Bristol Omnibus. By the time the company changed its name to Top Deck Travel in July 1983, a fleet of nearly 50 Lodekkas were owned and operated as Deckerhomes, including LD, FS and FLF type examples from the fleets of Alder Valley, Eastern National, Eastern Counties, Hants & Dorset, West Riding and Red & White, among others.

So what constitutes a Deckerhome, and what are they used for?

The exact layout of the Top Deck Travel Deckerhome is dictated to a certain extent by the vehicle concerned, as the LD and standard FS examples are rear entrance whilst the later FLF is forward entrance with driver operated doors. The lower deck is rebuilt with a sink unit on one side and a cooking area (fuelled by bottled gas) on the other, with storage cupboards being accommodated under both. The remainder of the lower deck incorporates coach seating and tables. The upper deck consists of eight permanent bunk beds, further seating and tables, and a concealed water tank which feeds the lower deck sink unit. Each vehicle also receives a stereo system and microphone with speakers throughout, and sufficient cupboard space for the stowage of luggage, spare fuel and tools and spares is provided.

Original fleet livery was cream with a central band of orange and black, although recent repaints have seen the introduction of cream livery with two diagonal orange and black stripes upswept towards the rear. Finally, each vehicle receives its distinctive name, which is hand-painted onto the front panel, often accompanied by a suitable logo. The choice of the name for each vehicle is a carefully thought out exercise: some vehicles receive names relevant to the history of the vehicle ("Deep Purple" was purple when acquired, "Phoenix" was rebuilt after fire damage), some are a reminder of the characteristics of Top Deck staff ("Sniffer" being a mechanic), whilst others are pure Australasian rhyming slang - enough said!

For over twenty years, Top Deck Travel (and formerly Argas Persicus) have been using Deckerhomes on long-haul continental expeditions throughout the World. Throughout the 1980s, a comprehensive selection of journeys ranging in duration from six weeks to six months was operated throughout Africa, South-East Asia and the Soviet Union, although Deckerhome operations within the United States were curtailed in 1986, largely due to access problems. Top Deck are particularly well known for pioneering the "Overland" journey to Kathmandu in Nepal, one of the most popular of the tourist trails that varies from eight to thirteen weeks in duration. Deckerhomes spend the majority of the year overseas, returning to their Surrey base for only a few months each winter. Once the buses are on mainland Europe, it is common for them to remain overseas for the entire season, with outward bound and return passengers being transferred to the British Channel Ports by feeder vehicles.

To many operators, this strategy would present major maintenance problems, but Top Deck has overcome this by providing all of its tour drivers with comprehensive mechanical training. If the driver is unable to repair his vehicle during an expedition, the company's Maintenance and Repair Centre at Horsell Common in Surrey will arrange for a replacement part to be flown to the vehicle within 24 hours. Extreme repairs have seen a Gardner diesel engine driven from Britain to the edge of the Sahara Desert, and then fitted with temperatures soaring above 100 degrees, and the story of a replacement Lodekka being driven in all haste to Kathmandu in Nepal to cover for a defective tour bus requires an article on its own.

The Maintenance and Repair Centre tracks all of the Top Deck Travel tours, by reports regularly sent by the tour driver. This not only means that the company knows exactly where all of its Deckerhomes are at any point, but means that the tour courier can be advised of any potential problems with the itinery. Problems and breakdowns with the Lodekkas are comparatively rare, largely due to a combination of the reliability of the vehicles, but also to the company's preventative maintenance policy which is effected at the Maintenance and Repair Centre.

The Lodekkas have proved to be ideal for this arduous lifestyle, and up until very recently, there were regular additions to the fleet as suitable examples became available. Top Deck has experimented with other types of vehicles in the past, notably a batch of Moseley-bodied Ford coaches in the late 1970s and 14 assorted Bristol VRTs between 1981 and 1986. The VRs were not entirely successful as Deckerhomes, and several were operated only as tour shuttle vehicles within Britain. Both the Fords and the Bristol VRs were only short-term residents within the Top Deck fleet. More recently a pair of VanHool bodied Scania executive coaches have been employed to cover Ski Top Deck commitments to European ski resorts, as well as an ever increasing private hire requirement.

Since 1990, the Lodekka fleet has slowly declined in strength to meet the changing demands for Top Deck's tours. Several of the oldest Lodekkas have been sold (some for preservation), whilst others have been cannibalised at Horsell Common to replenish the company's extensive store of spares. It is unlikely that any further examples will be added to the fleet, and Top Deck Travel are seeking an alternative vehicle capable of undertaking this challenging and demanding work. Current investigations are concentrating on the possibility of mounting a coach body on the rear of a Mercedes 17-ton flat bed truck. One trial conversion has already been completed, and the prototype is still hard at work in the Andes and the Amazon jungle in South America.

The Top Deck Lodekka, however, will remain active for many years to come - a living reminder of the Great British bus industry which we can but mourn the demise of today. As you are reading this, there are Deckerhomes going about their daily business of transporting tourists and travellers to the far corners of the World. Spare a thought for these distinctive orange and cream continental drifters, or just dream of all the places that they regularly visit that you probably never will . . . . .

Top Deck's latest acquisition is "Phoenix", which arrived from the fleet of Silcox, Pembroke Dock in 1992. Rightfully registered KGH 891A (new as 804 SHW), it is seen here en route for Dover in 1993 temporarily carrying the registration from "Rags".

Deckerhome Lodekka YHT 932 (Hulk) is seen here taking a break whilst journeying through Central India. New to the Bristol Omnibus Company, this particular vehicle has given many years service on overland expeditions to Kathmandu in Nepal.

Top Deck has operated several of the rarer FS6G-type Lodekkas as Deckerhomes. New to Hants & Dorset, 4382 LJ rests at Mayford in Surrey before the 1990 season.

Lower deck view of FLJ 155D - "Deep Purple" - Deckerhome conversion.

Only during the winter months do all of Top Deck Travel's Lodekkas return to their native country. VGS 375 awaits sunnier climates at Mayford, Surrey in February 1990.

"Freckle", HPN 79D, is unique in carrying a white-based livery instead of cream. This Deckerhome was new to Brighton, Hove & District but was acquired from Alder Valley District.

Upper deck view of FLJ 155D - "Deep Purple" - Deckerhome conversion.

◄ One of Top Deck's two Vanhool bodied Scania coaches, G39 KHY, is seen at Pas De Las Casa, Andora (8,101 feet) fitted with snow chains, whilst operating a ski Top Deck holiday.

A trio of former Southern Vectis Lodekkas: "Drab", "Lemming" and "Befa" pose for the photographer at Goreme in Eastern Turkey during an overnight stop in May 1989.

"Drab" (PDL 517) makes an overnight stop at a picturesque stretch of Turkish coastline during a 1989 overland expedition.

On-board advertising for "Boogie" - LD6G Lodekka ODL 11.

Deckerhome PDL 517 "Drab" receives mechanical attention at Kathmandu in 1988, before the return journey of its overland expedition.

"Golly" (DAL 309C) seen here at Southampton Docks prior to 1983, was destroyed by fire at Horsell Common in April 1990. A 1965 Bristol FLF6G with ECW bodywork she was acquired from East Midlands (ex 454) in 1977.

[D. Stevenson]

One of Top Deck's original Deckerhomes was "Boogie" - formerly Southern Vectis LD6G Lodekka ODL 11. After over 15 years of transcontinental expeditions, "Boogie" was re-registered to APB 712A and sold in early 1993.

— Busy Bus —

BUSY BUS 1

The Birmingham & Midland Motor Omnibus Company built class SOS or 'Standard' vehicles were to become out-of-date very quickly, not because of any inherent fault but because bodywork styling changed. The 4.3 litre engines as supplied to Trent were sturdy and reliable so it was logical in 1930, when they were four years old, that the entire batch of 32 were rebodied by United, predecessors of Eastern Coachworks (E.C.W.). Thus refurbished, and reclassified ODD they survived for another six years on lightly loaded country routes.

BUSY BUS 2

Looking remarkably clean and smart for a Walsall Corporation omnibus No. 115 (MDH 323) was one of a pair of Guy Arab III chassis powered by the Gardner 5LW (5 cylinders-Light Weight) first supplied in 1949 with this unusual Park Royal 56 seat bodywork. It seems that these chassis were never intended to receive these bodies and indeed both the style and quality are far better than most bus bodies supplied to Walsall. However, it also appears to be an uncomfortable fit. After fourteen years service she was withdrawn in August 1963 and converted to a driver training vehicle, being used for this purpose until May 1964. Later that year she passed to a dealer and worked for a contractor for an unknown length of time.

Behind is one of their 'Best Buys' an ex London Transport Leyland 7RT OLD 596 ex RTL 1487, Walsall's 203, built in 1954 with a Park Royal 56 seat body, markedly different to that of 115. After only five years with LT RTL 1487 was found to be 'in excess of requirements' but served the Corporation well until the formation of the West Midlands P.T.E. on 1 October 1969, when she was renumbered 203L. Never repainted into PTE livery she was far too unorthodox for their taste and sold to Wombwell Diesels for scrap in November 1971.

BUSY BUS 3

Chieftain (J. Lawrie & Company of Hamilton) bought 26 ex Birmingham Corporation Transport vehicles between 1952 and 1956, but few had such an unusual life as FOF 307, seen here sometime in 1954. Delivered in 1939 as No. 1307 she had a Leyland 52 seat standard body modified to BCT requirements on a TD6c 'gearless' chassis, developed with a fluid coverter for the easy conversion of redundant tramwaymen to bus drivers - more or less the same job the Tillings-Stevens petrol-electrics had been designed for twenty years earlier.

Officially withdrawn in 1951, FOF 307 was sold to Chieftain in 1952 where as No. 44 she was to serve them well on services between Hamilton and East Kilbride until 1960. By then, 21 years old, she might have gone to the bus graveyard but instead her body was removed from the chassis, overhauled and placed on the chassis of ex-Yorkshire Woollen District HD 7826 itself a 1942 Leyland PD2/1 whose Brush body was rotten. This had been sold to a dealer near Rugby in January 1960, and had been transported to Edinburgh in July. In October 1961 Chieftain became part of the Central SMT group, 'our' vehicle by now No. 70, was disposed of in June 1962 for further service with St. Andrews Church, Dunkeld, where she was still in existance in May 1966, 27 years after Leyland craftsmen built the body for Birmingham, and 24 years after the chassis entered service in Yorkshire.

Visible by her bonnet is the bus stop which advised passengers to queue for Farm Road, Belhave Road and Comely Law. The Monarchs were racing against Bristol Bulldogs at the Edinburgh Stadium and you are exhorted to drink McEwans, suck Smarties (wotalot I got) and to smoke Batchelor cigarettes.

1

2

BUSY BUS 4

JDH 33 (fleet number 221) was one of a series of Guy Arab II chassis with Park Royal utility 56-seat bodywork and Gardner 5-cylinder engines delivered in 1943. As was Walsall's wont various of that years intake suffered changes in either engine or bodywork but 221 was a special case. John Reohorn picks up the story:

Are you aware of the story behind JDH 33's mutilation? It concerns Bentley, a suburb of Darlaston and situated on Walsall's boundary (Bentley Hill figured in Charles II's escape and the Wesley Riots). In the 50's it was being developed for housing. Walsall put in several new routes, but one estate on Bentley Hill was left out. There is a very low bridge at the Darlaston end of this road, too low for even the Bedfords. Accordingly Birchills workshops cut down a utility. However the traffic commissioners would have nothing to do with the scheme, the bus failed to get a certificate of fitness and so it ended its days as a static canteen in Bradford Place, replacing an elderly Dennis Ace that had begun the role during the war. The photo (1) shows it in its purpose built bay, originally it stood at the rear of the passenger stands. (2)

BUSY BUS 5

Although the registration of Western SMT's vehicle 2295 may sound like a bus ticket this was in fact a somewhat uncommon Guy-bodied Guy Arab III. It did not roam far from the territory of its original owner, Paisley & District Omnibus Company (an 'associate' of Young's Bus Service Ltd) nonetheless XS 6557 (Paisley's 295) was delivered in 1949, nationalized in June 1950 when it passed into the ownership of the British Transport Commission who in turn handed the vehicle over to Western in 1951, so this Guy had, on paper, three owners in as many years.

Allocated to Johnstone garage, 2295 was always outstationed at Paisley and is seen on a local route. Still with its original 56-seat Guy body this elegant bus was withdrawn in 1963.

BUSY BUS 6

HGC 148 started life in 1945 when complete with Weymann semi-utility 56 seat body she was one of 299 Guy Arabs, 148 Daimler CW and 20 Bristol K6A chassis delivered to London Transport between the beginning of 1945 and the Spring of 1946. A typical Guy Arab II the high-set radiator and sawn-off wings distinguish her from XS 6557, a postwar Mk. III. Irregardless of the condition of her bodywork, the sad facts were that by 1950 London Transport drivers were not going to tolerate rigid mounted Gardner engines with all their noise, heat and vibration coupled to a crash gearbox when with a little persistence they knew an AEC Regent (RT class) with pre-select box and 'floating' engine could be allocated. And after a peak in 1948 there could not be any doubt that passenger figures were falling and more comfort and greater service speed were required to steady this. So the Arabs went - declining from 370 in 1950 to 1 in 1952. And HGC 148 (one time G 369) was one of them, being sold to Western SMT via a dealer in 1951, then running out of Dumfries Garage for a while without a fleet number until she received her new Alexander L27/26 bodywork and number 1006 the following year. Apparently Western drivers were hardier men than their London counterparts, HGC 148 remaining in service until 1963, when perhaps a little improbably she was purchased by Highland Omnibus who had another four years work out of a once despised 1945 chassis.

BUSY BUS 7

Although this bus, seen in its midlife manifestation did not wander too far, it certainly underwent some vicissitudes during its lifetime.

The majority of traditional PSV's were built in two or three layers, a bit like 'angel' cake. The bottom was the chassis plus powerpack, the lower deck or saloon the middle lump and the upper deck or smoking saloon the topmost layer. These three components can be split and the power pack can have engine/transmission changes almost at will.

In 1931 the Tyneside Tramroads & Tramways Company took delivery of VK 3840 a Leyland TD1 with Duple 55 seat bodywork which they sold to Barton Transport of Chilwell in 1941 where it became their No. 411. Given that ten years was the normal life of a bus in those days it is not surprising that a few years later the chassis was worn out, but remarkably after some refurbishment the body was placed on a new Leyland PD1 chassis in 1947 and re-registered HRR 942, No. 455.

However in 1953 the body itself failed and a new one was fitted to the 1947 chassis not, however, before this was lengthened. Re-numbered 669 and re-registered NVO 266 it was supplied with a 39 seat *coach* body!

BUSY BUS 8

From April 1954 to March 1967 SAU 199 led the normal life of a city service bus in Nottingham. Like most of her kind for a few weeks she was a garage 'pet', but after a dent or two 199, an AEC Regent III with Park Royal 53 seat low-height body, became just another member of the fleet until she was sold to Bartons, as their number 1087. But it was after disposal from them to a dealer in August 1972 that SAU 199 really became a wandering bus as, given a repaint in red and the addition of London Transport lettering, she was exported to the United States of America in October 1972, remaining in existance for at least a decade. [J. Fozard]

— Aspects of Advertising —

SELLING THE VEHICLE

From a series of advertisements some of the story of Public Service Vehicle evolution becomes clear. And, too, in the pages of old transport magazines are often the last dreams of companies long gone. Hurst Nelson showed their curiosity with its forward mounted emergency exit in 1934; AEC their Regents in the following year while just postwar (1946) Foden were hoping for fleet orders and in 1954 Park Royal showed designs of which two would not be so out-of-place today.

But out of all these advertisers only one exists in any form and they have changed hands. Hurst Nelson failed to secure large orders and as trams and steam trains went so did they. AEC were 'rationalized' out of business, while Sheffield Corporation have long lost their fleet of buses to the P.T.E. Foden remain, but have not built bus chassis since the ill-fated Foden-NC. And of the Park Royal-Roe partnership nothing remains except Optare who at least keep part of the Roe works open. The worst part for the historian was the side effect of this as transport magazines, heavily dependent on advertising, saw major companies fading away. As they did, so did many of the component manufacturers and as the advertisements went, so did the PSV magazines.

HURST NELSON & CO., LTD.

Builders and Repairers of

RAILWAY CARRIAGES - WAGONS - ELECTRIC CARS

and every other description of

RAILWAY AND TRAMWAY ROLLING STOCK

MOTOR OMNIBUS AND OTHER ROAD VEHICLE BODIES

The Glasgow Rolling Stock and Plant Works

MOTHERWELL

London Office: 32, GREAT ST. HELEN'S, BISHOPSGATE, E.C.3. Glasgow Office: 78, ST. VINCENT STREET, C.2.

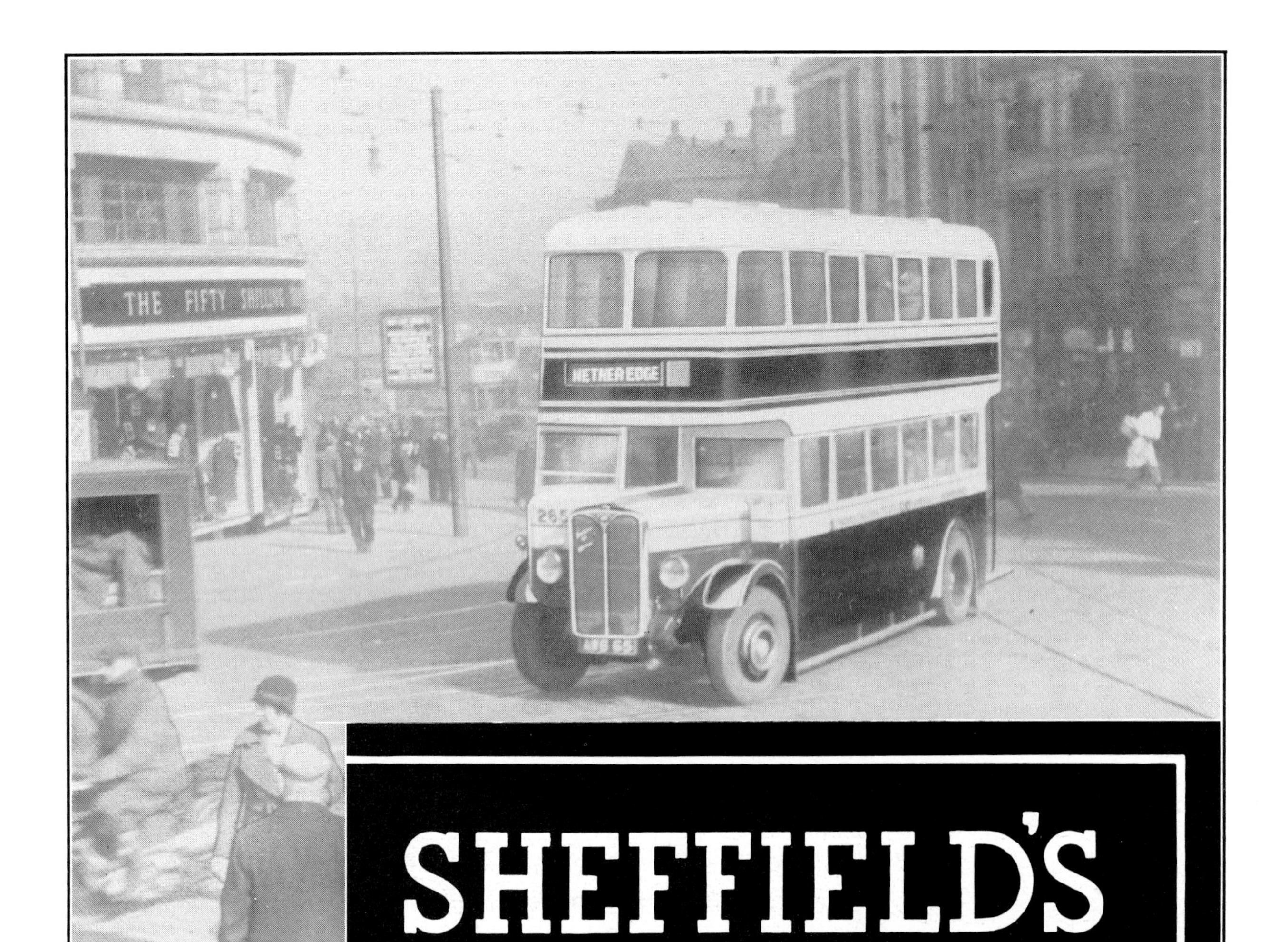

NEW OIL-ENGINED "REGENTS"

PASSENGER VEHICLES
OIL OR PETROL

Depicted above is one of the fleet of A.E.C. "Regent" double deckers recently placed in service by the Sheffield Transport Department. These vehicles, powered by the popular A.E.C.-Ricardo 130 h.p. 6 cyl. oil engines, are also equipped with fluid transmission systems. Thus has Sheffield enhanced its civic prestige and assured the efficiency of its public service transport by operating Britain's predominating passenger vehicles.

We shall be pleased to send details of the A.E.C. passenger range and 4 and 6 cylinder oil engines on request.

THE ASSOCIATED EQUIPMENT Co. LTD. SOUTHALL, MDX
BUILDERS OF LONDON'S BUSES

2244

the 'double-decker' with a great name

There's ninety years of superlative design, fine workmanship and hard experience behind this latest addition to the Foden range.

The new Double-Decker is in every way worthy of carrying on the proud name and trusted tradition that has made Fodens pre-eminent in the world of road transport. And there's a "Single-Decker," too, that is equally attractive.

FODENS LTD · SANDBACH · CHESHIRE

PARK ROYAL VEHICLES LTD
Extend to all their friends Sincere Wishes for a Happy Christmas and a Prosperous New Year
1955
EAST KENT
BIRCH
NORTHERN
ALL THAT IS BEST IN COACHWORK
PARK ROYAL VEHICLES LTD
PARK ROYAL · LONDON · ENGLAND PHONE: ELGAR 6522

More and more coaches are carrying the distinctive Radiomobile aerial that signifies Coach Radio at its best—

"HIS MASTER'S VOICE"

AUTOMOBILE RADIO & SPEECH AMPLIFICATION EQUIPMENT FOR PASSENGER VEHICLES

Product of

RADIOMOBILE LTD., CRICKLEWOOD WORKS
CRICKLEWOOD, LONDON, N.W.2

COACH OPERATORS

write for the name of your nearest Radiomobile Accredited Dealer and full particulars of "His Master's Voice" Automobile Radio and Speech Amplification Equipment for Passenger Vehicles.

HALL & NIELSEN LTD · Beaver Mills · Bury · Lancs · Eng

PHONE · BURY · 953 ★ ★ ★ GRAMS · 'BRAKES' · BURY

ADVERTISING SELLS

Not only should it sell, but it *must* sell the product to keep the factory running. All these advertisements appeared over two years 1949-1951, during the so-called 'era of austerity', and represent a fair cross-section through the components advertised as being available.

Although all the items (except the radio, perhaps) could be called essential it is interesting to see that Oldham emphasise the revenue gaining benefits of good lighting. It cannot be coincidental that both brake lining companies use night time for their illustrations, and appeal to the after market, i.e. the maintenance engineer, whereas Ferodo wanted to be specified for new build.

FERODO STAIRTREADS may be expected to retain their safe, non-slip surface throughout the useful life of the vehicle to which they are fitted.

The aluminium nosing clearly outlines each step, while the inlaid strips of Ferodo fabric, non-slip through and through, seem to absorb endless wear without themselves wearing appreciably. They give a firm, safe tread, even to wet shoes. Passengers move confidently, time is saved at stops.

Ferodo Stairtreads are easily adapted and fitted to all stair and step designs. A special type without metal backing is available to comply with trolley-bus regulations. We shall be pleased to send our descriptive catalogue No. 732 FF on request, and to give any further information or advice.

FERODO
STAIRTREADS

FERODO LIMITED, CHAPEL-EN-LE-FRITH
A Member of the Turner & Newall Organization

Improved Anti-Rattler for Ventilators

GAGE'S PATENT.

This arrangement as illustrated, has been specially designed for Hinged Ventilators, and meet a long felt want. It entirely prevents rattling over the roughest road on any vehicle. It is entirely dust-proof, neat in appearance, low in price, and has nothing to get out of order.

It consists of a small Tube in which is fitted a Piston or Plunger, and at the back a coiled Spring which is kept in position by a Hexagon Cap or Nut.

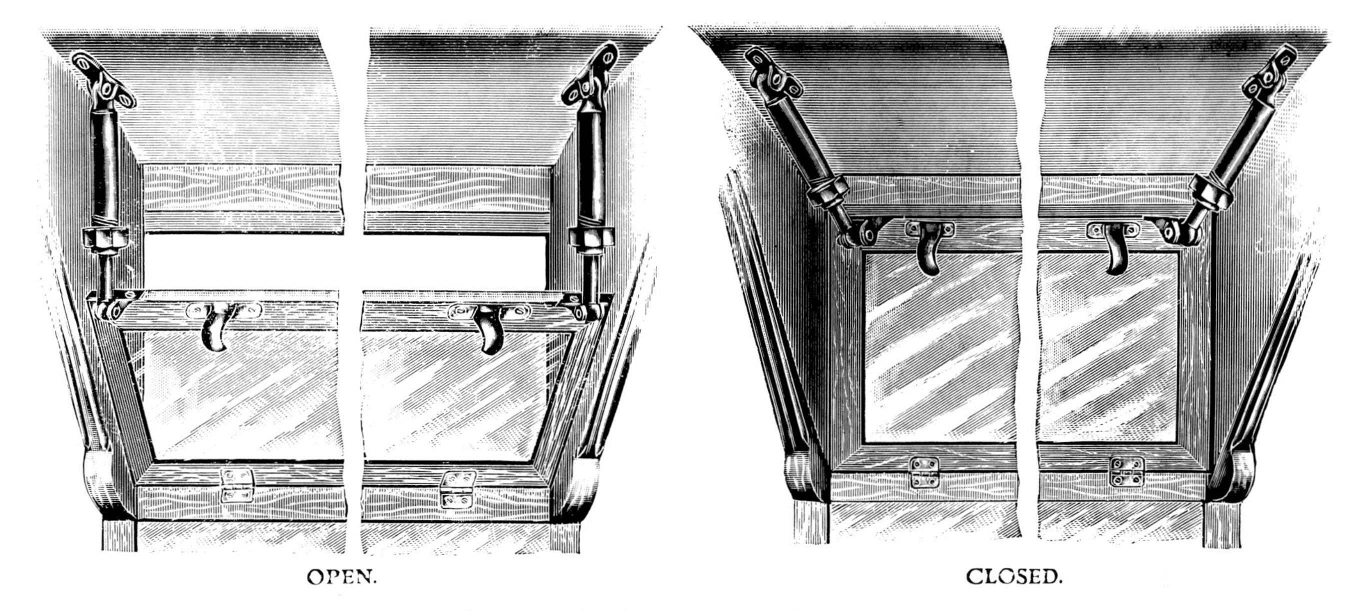

OPEN. CLOSED.

At the one end of the fitting is placed an angle Bracket for attaching to the Ventilator Frame, and at the other end a Bracket for fixing to the Roof, and these are supplied Right or Left Hand.

It is so designed that the Ventilator is firmly fixed when open or shut, and no other catch or fastening is required, and it is easily opened by a slight pull, or closed by the pressure of the hand.

It is specially recommended for the Ventilators in Motor 'Buses, Trolley 'Buses, Tram Cars, Railway Carriages, and can be used for Side or Roof Ventilators.

The above illustrations show a Ventilator open and shut in one of the Birmingham Corporation 'Buses, and wherever fixed has given every possible satisfaction. 16,000 pairs alone have been supplied to the London General Omnibus Company.

Price **1/6** (One Shilling and Sixpence) each.

Sole Manufacturers:

GABRIEL & CO.,

A B Row, Birmingham.

Manufacturers of Tramcar Fittings, Motor Car and Motor 'Bus Fittings, Railway Carriage Fittings, &c.

Contractors to the Admiralty, War Office, Air Board, India Office, Crown Agents for the Colonies, and the leading English, Colonial and Foreign Railways and Corporations.

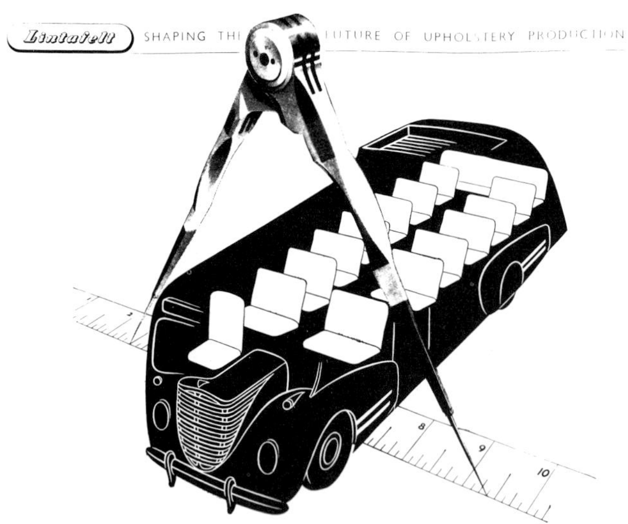

Measuring up to production targets

LINTAFELT MADE-TO-MEASURE upholstery pads are solving a multitude of labour, storage and waste problems. Modern production is demanding modern methods to combat rising costs and competition.
PRE-MADE FILLINGS are supplied by Lintafelt to manufacturers' specifications cut to any size or shape, constructed of Lintafelt or Lintafelt and fibre mounted on a hessian base, all encased in muslin, if desired, with ready-to-fix flies, for wood or metal frames.
SAVINGS in overheads and production costs more than offset the initial cost of prefabrication.
CUTTING PRODUCTION TIME by as much as 60%, Lintafelt methods are being increasingly adopted in the upholstery and allied trades.
IMPROVING THE FINISHED PRODUCT.
Lintafelt (a blend of cotton and cotton linters) filling is made only from new raw material. Hygenic and durable, its layer structure obviates 'shifting' and 'lumping'; and its exceptional resiliency prodives that luxury comfort demanded by passengers at home and abroad.
LINTAFELT RESEARCH AND DEVELOPMENT DEPT. is at the service of manufacturers and technicians to co-operate in solving all upholstery and production problems.

The Lintafelt advertisement dates from 1950 when there was strong competition both between manufacturers of seats and the suppliers of materials. The Geon/Distillers advertisement appeared January 1962, while the Dapta (Accles & Pollock) seat brochure was issued in the mid-1950s.

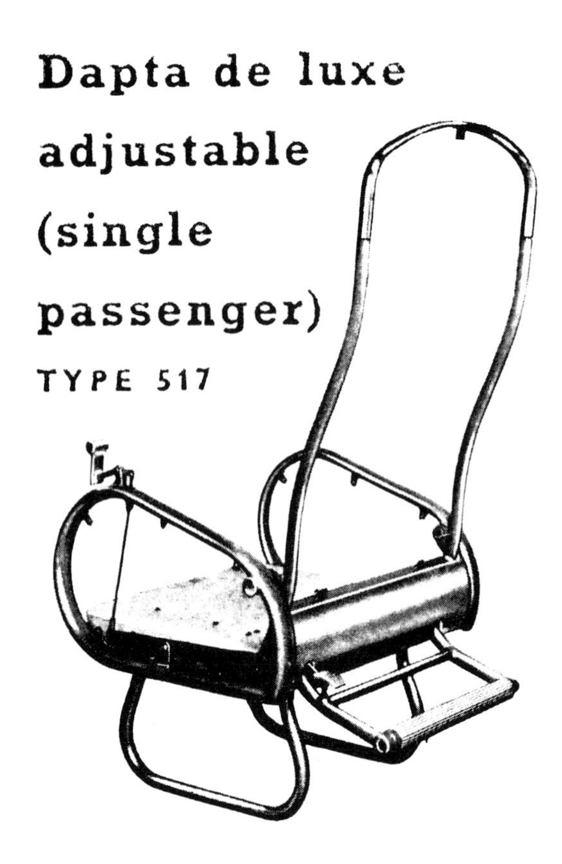

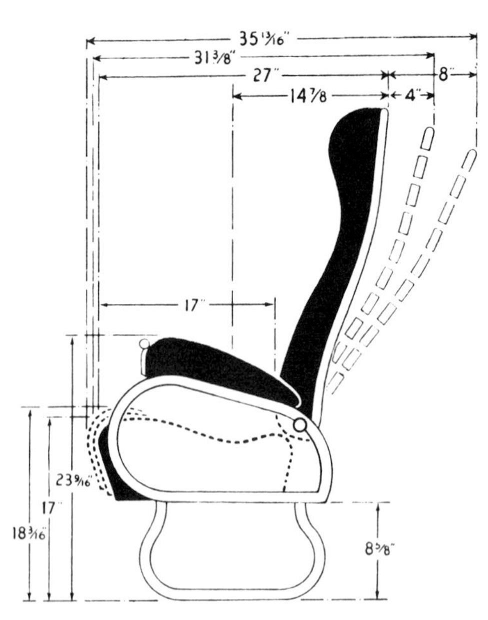

Seat and back position adjustable, finger control on arm rest. Applicable for both the 517 and 493 models.

BEAUTIES SELLING

Advertising on passenger carrying vehicles goes back at least 250 years as it was common practice for the operators of horse-drawn 'Flying Machines' to carry their names and addresses on the tail-boards of their wagons. Additionally some had an early form of slip-board giving details of their operations, these being mounted on the topraves or on the canvas tilt. Stagecoaches were famous for their advertisements and in a way represented the 'Company' vehicles of their day, as opposed to the Royal Mail coaches, who like the 'Municipals' (at least early on) were quite unadorned.

Only short captions are given for this collection but it is interesting to see how, even in the last forty years the nature of the advertisements has changed from the simple paper sticker to todays all-over themes. The only problem with some of the latter is to see where the wretched bus is going, especially in a strange town where the passenger has to contend with different blind layouts.

Beware!

Self-Advertising adjacent to Stratford-upon-Avon railway station.

Justified self advertising.

Aftermath of a strike. Good advertisement but poor presentation at Bexley Heath.
(W.J. Haynes)

80 years of Todmorden buses, but not now a proud Municipal.

The Tunnel represented progress, the 1929 Thornycroft did not.

Local radio, a beer and National bus.
(G. Pickard)

The Crossley lasted 15 years, Vernons rather longer, the roadworks seemingly forever.

Solid fuel sold the discreet way one advertised in the 1960s.

Bradford, land of trams, trolleybuses, motor-buses and by 1986 the 'Metrobus'.

Local radio and all rather cheerful.
(G. Pickard)

It always seems a bit odd to advertise a Motor dealer.

And garish seems right for the 1980s.

Food 1950 style.

Food 1985 style. (G. Pickard)

Change of customer, but food nontheless 1992.

Food of life, Derby style.

Food of life, London style.

Bit sad really. 'Nelson' cigarettes are gone, real money gone, trolleybus 1270 has long gone, pure Leyland chassis are no longer built and Leyland body-building is a fading memory.

Clever advertisement seen at a rally.

Clear advert but dreadful destination blind. The bus didn't belong to the newspaper but Colchester Borough Transport.

The Police try hard to spread the message.
(Daniel Hill Photography)

And combined with Centro to do so in the West Midlands.

In modern parlance this could be said to be 'utterly laid-back' advertising. Daimler Roadliner with Plaxton body photographed at the demonstration park, Earls Court Motor Show, 1968.

STRANGE SURVIVAL

In 1963 Guy Motors of Wolverhampton built one of the handful of demonstrators they ever found necessary (7 in all since the war, where Daimler had 14, and Ford 30!). This was for the then-new chassis type Arab V using build No. FD 75320 but with an example of rare Strachans 72 double deck bodywork. This was rather strange in outline and painted in an approximation of Halifax Corporation style, being loaned to them in 1964 after appearing at the 1963 Scottish Motor Show, although no orders resulted, 888 DUK in due course being sold to the Midlands operator Harper Brothers of Heath Hayes. Following the acquisition of the company by Midland Red in 1974 the Arab became redundant and was scrapped at the yard. There the story might have ended had not one of Harper's drivers sold this builders plate recently, it turning out to be none other than that from 888 DUK - body No. M.3831. Surely a survival against all odds.

Perhaps there may still be something in Mr Tony Weller's words to his son, Sam, in Pickwick:

"Cos a coachman's a priviledged indiwidual" replied Mr Weller, looking fixedly at his son "Cos a coachman may do vithout suspicion wot other men may not, 'cos a coachman may be on the wery amicablest terms with eighty mile of females, and yet nobody think that he ever means to marry any vun among them".

FROM JOHN HIBBS "COUNTRY BUS". DAVID & CHARLES 1986

CO-ORDINATED COLOURS

Halifax Corporation operated trams until 1939, although they had begun to phase them out in 1931. Motorbus operation started in 1912 but in 1929 a Joint Committee was formed between the Corporation, London Midland & Scottish and the London & North Eastern Railways whereby, in effect, they cut up the area between them. The services within the borough were to remain in the hands of the Corporation, the outer suburban routes would be worked by the Corporation on behalf of the Joint Committee, and the longer, virtually inter-urban services would be handled by the railways.

The story of their light green, orange and cream livery is well known but deserves repeating, as it was the result of the merest fluke with the then Committee viewing the Glasgow Corporation colours in which an AEC Regent demonstrator was painted in 1929, and promptly adopting them! And the vehicle was good, too, Halifax buying nothing other than AECs until 1940.

Interestingly and uncommonly the legal lettering on the side of this brand new Charles Roberts of Sheffield bodied 1937 Regent reads "Joint Omnibus Committee, Halifax Corporation Motors" and the crest "Joint Committee, Halifax Corporation & Railway Services".

The second illustration shows a 1950 AEC Regent III No.377, with Park Royal bodywork now preserved, and entering Dartmouth Park, Sandwell in May 1990. At least we can still listen to the sound and see the colours of a 'Joint Committee' vehicle.

SELLING BEAUTY

The Great Western Railway first sent out an advertising bus in 1905 and by 1907 a Milnes-Daimler from Paignton had reached as far north as Inverness, covering some 2,500 miles; more of a monument to the stamina of the drivers than any real value, despite extolling the scenic virtues of the Vale of Llangollen, Cornish Riviera, Bala, Barmouth and the Severn Tunnel route. This 45 h.p. AEC No. 259 (XK 9102) seen here with a Great Western bus body was new in May 1922 with a charabanc body but during the winter of 1925/6 was sent off, as shown, on a tour to publicize the company.

During the early 1920s there was a great demand for mini-bus or mini-coach type vehicles. They were, and today are, ideal for wedding parties, christenings and small private excursions. Normally based on Ford chassis various converters lengthened and strengthened the underframe and provided a body, often for a ridiculously low price. This offering from Baico (who still function today) was dated 1922. Interestingly they alone offered the correct plural tense for our misused 'Franglais' char-a-banc, albeit then advertising an all-weather saloon. Almost every Midland company either started with or purchased one or more of these ultra-lightweights; they commonly appear in 1920 snapshots of Aunt Ada and her cronies.

BAICO

STANDARD 20 SEATER

CHARS-A-BANCS DE LUXE

" The public conveyance with the appearance and actual comfort of a private limousine."

20-SEATER BAICO ALL-WEATHER SALOON BODY.

SPECIFICATION.

Framing and bearers of oak. Steel panels throughout with three-ply lining. All corners rounded into graceful lines. Interior seating accommodation for 20 persons—17 in back and 3 in front, in addition to driver. Handsomely upholstered best quality leather cloth spring seats, with wide back rest arranged across body with passage up centre.

Three-ply canvas-covered roof, supported by combined wood and steel pillars. Back panels brought up to join roof smoothly. Doors each side driver's seat, with glass windows to drop half way. Glass side windows detachable or fixed as desired. Oval glass windows in rear end of body. Windscreen substantially built up from dash with half of top part arranged to open in front of driver. Electric ceiling light in interior of body, electric head and rear and oil side lamps, with self-starting type engine. The whole beautifully painted and finished to choice.

GENERAL DIMENSIONS:

Over-all length	17 ft. 0 in.
Over-all height	8 ft. 3 in.
Over-all width	6 ft. 6 in.
Height from platform to roof	5 ft. 4 in.

BAICO PATENTS, LIMITED

115, FULHAM ROAD, LONDON, S.W. 3

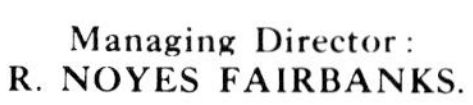

Managing Director:
R. NOYES FAIRBANKS.

A PANORAMIC VIEW OF THE PLAXTON PANORAMA

Until a few years ago the Plaxton Panorama coach or express bus body was commonplace on British roads both on front line and contract or school duties.

The earliest version, exemplified by photograph 1 was derived from their 'Consort' design and appeared in 1958. The primary difference between this and extant models like the 'Consort' lay in the substitution of three main 'picture' windows per side in lieu of 5 or 6; a remarkable increase in light and viewing area immediately becoming apparent. In this 1959 photograph of a Panorama body on an AEC Reliance chassis the kick-up of the rear is visible as are the three windows at the back and the split windscreen.

Although a 1951 chassis this Leyland Royal Tiger, lengthened and fitted with the then new Panorama body in 1959, was the runner-up at the National Coach Rally, Blackpool, 1964. A one-piece windscreen has appeared.

[Vintage Roadscene Publications Ltd.]

3

A 1960 AEC Reliance stands alongside a Guy LUF with Seagull bodywork. The rather sad Panorama grill was ostensibly for the 1961 season, together with the 'cross-eyed' light clusters. The contrast in glazed area between the two bodies is remarkable.

4

AWA 349B one of four 1964 AEC Reliance coaches obtained by Bedlington & District from Sheffield United Tours in November 1975 is included to show the distortion of the boot area found towards the end of a Panorama body's life.

5

1963 47-seat body on Leyland Leopard chassis. The impression of length, helped by the sloping waistline, is impressive.

6

For the 1965 season heavy revision of the design was undertaken; the chrome area of the first bay now reducing the impact of length.

[Michael Allen]

7

Midland Red has 16 bodies of this design fitted to Leyland Leopard chassis in 1965/6 (1 class LC8, 15 LC9) but due to their low seating capacity the LC9s were withdrawn 1976, some being converted to breakdown trucks as shown here, still in service in 1993. The differences in door design with that in photos 1 and 5 is marked.

8

In 1965 Plaxtons decided that all their new bodies, irregardless of chassis type or detail would be known as Panorama. (Mk) I had fixed windows and ram-air ventilation, (Mk) II more traditional top sliders. One of the latter is seen here, showing vastly simplified trim.

And on a longer, Bedford VAM 14 chassis the 1978, 41 seat variant is seen in 1992.

Back end detail.

In 1968 came the Panoramic Elite, with curved side glasses and although stainless steel trim has returned it is with a purpose. This, presumably occupied, vehicle was found rather eerily lurking in a field at Ollerton, near Blyth, Nottingham, during 1993. The luggage rack was fitted for continental travel.

12

◄ Sporting a Northern Irish registration this AEC Reliance carries the 1969 Elite body. It was and is considered by some reviewers that the true Panorama body ended with the introduction of the Elite styling, but the long deep windows are still there.

13

Photographed at the start of the British Coach Rally, Epsom Downs, 18 April 1970, classical Leopard chassis with Elite bodywork. The extra roof lights are to distinguish the vehicle in a crowded coach park while the wireless aerial is unusually mounted in the roof.

[S.W. Stevens-Stratten]

Variation. The chassis is a 1973 AEC Reliance but the body has 'bus grant' power-operated folding doors. Designated Panorama Express this alternative and a few other minor modification enabled an operator with stage-carriage (express) work to recover up to 50% of the vehicles' prime cost. Seen at a rally in 1990. In 1970 the Elite progressed to a (Mk) II model, mainly in relation to the trim, but the (Mk) III of 1972 - the last Panorama even in name - had many alterations especially involving the rear light fittings and again the side trim was re-arranged. ➤

14

15

▲Ford chassis, Panorama Elite III bodywork new 1975. Seen on a filthy wet day 1992.

16

▲And the rather severe back contrasting with photograph 10.

17

▲Ford again but 1974, Panorama Elite III. Photograph 1993. Used as a rally-attending 'touring home'. ▼

18

19

◄ To add piquancy here is another Bedlington & District (ex S.U.T.) 1964 Panorama bodied AEC Reliance, emphasizing ten years of panoramic evolution.

20

21

The contrast was even more marked in the interior, when the fussy arrangement of a late Consort body is compared with a 3-bay (albeit very early) Panorama.

— Bell Punch To Almex —

BELL PUNCH VARIETY

The Bell Punch ticket is probably one of the best known in the world. Their machines (and the Williamson equivalent) were tough, reliable and in the days of the conductor quite efficient. In normal times they could be purchased or leased but by November 1943 it was a case of 'make do and mend'.

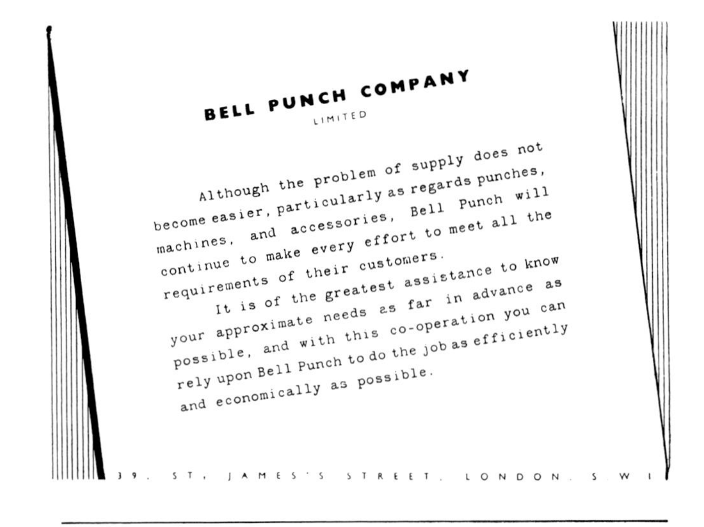

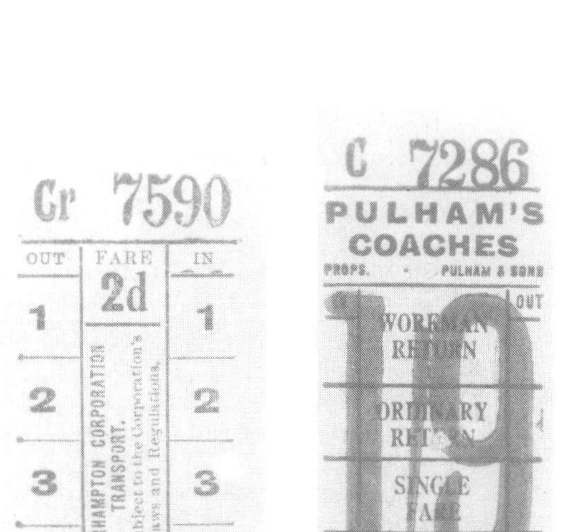

Green

Grey, Red overprint

Grey-blue
Blue overprint

Beige/blue
1/6 red

Beige/pink
3/- blue

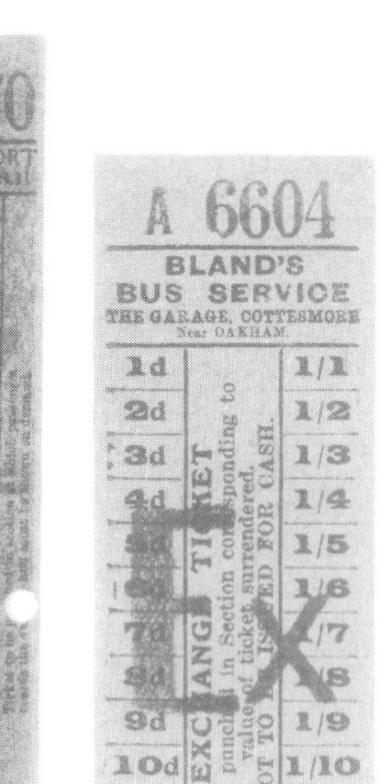

Two-tone Orange
Green overprint

Orange
red overprint

Sage green
Red overprint

Grey-green
Red overprint

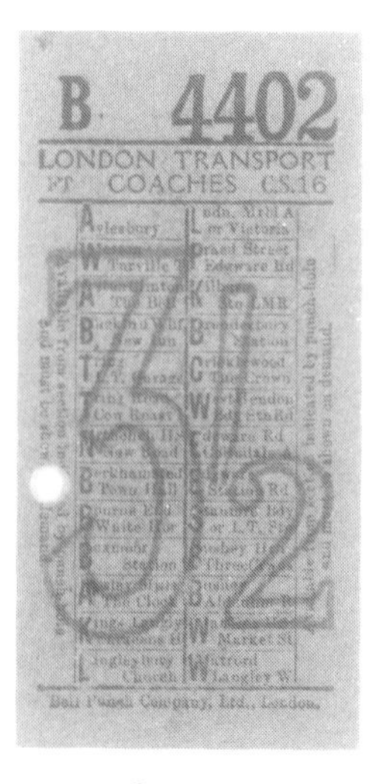

Orange
Green overprint

Unless otherwise stated, all lettering is black.

COMMEMORATIVE TICKETS

Collecting commemorative bus and coach tickets can be a fascinating subject on its own, taking little space, requiring positively no garage, oil, water, diesel or even a valid licence and yet you have the excuse to go to rallies which no-one can deny you!

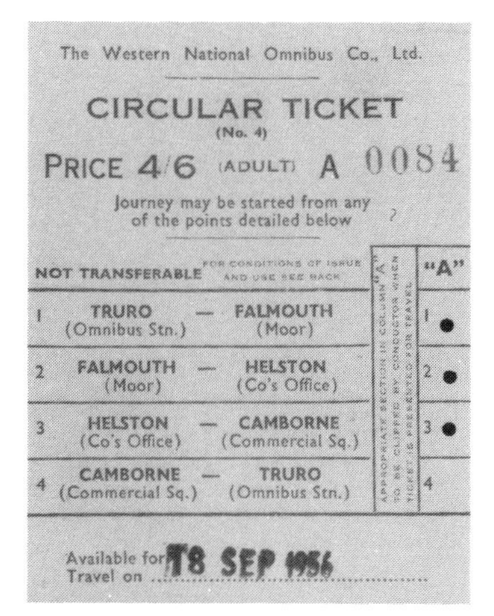

75mm x 90mm, Pink.
Reverse quotes conditions.

75mm x 85mm, colour blue

60mm x 90mm, blue and gold endorsed "This ticket may be retained as a souvenir".

100mm x 150mm, blue. Timetable on back

80mm x 170mm, Yellow

The sheer volume of tickets issued and the ephemeral nature tends to mean certain types are easily found, while the less orthodox get thrown away.

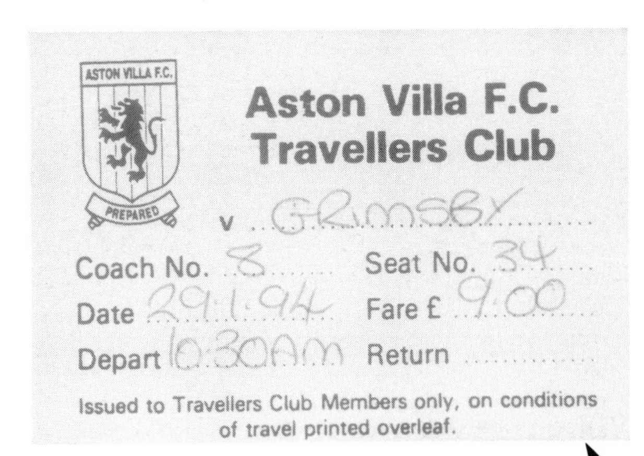

Measuring 90mm x 60mm this represents a very special ticket. Whether one would want to travel by Central Liner after seeing this is a matter of taste, although it is rare to find a service coach full of football supporters!

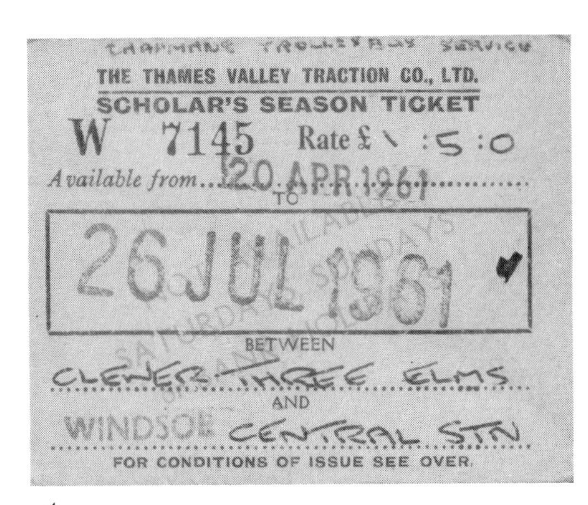

Two school bus specials. The endorsement on the Thames Valley one (not available Saturdays, Sundays and Bank Holidays) is interesting as locally one regularly finds youths travelling on this type of ticket on a Saturday and claiming they are going to swimming lessons/choir practice/marathon running when they clearly are not, but it cannot be proved they are not!

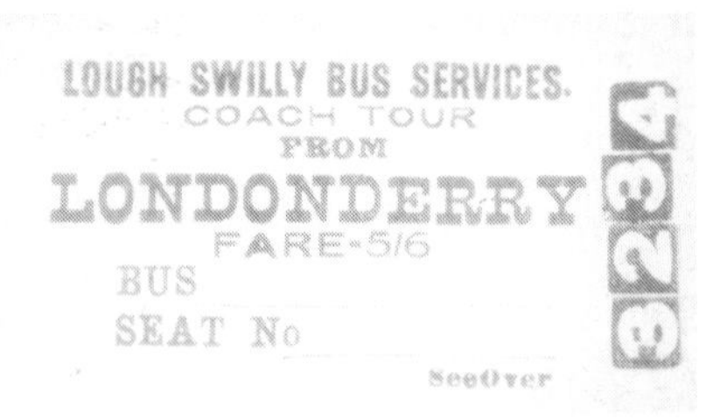

◄For use in the event of machines failure, all conductors carried packs of 'Bell Punch' tickets and could use the punch on some Setright machines to endorse them, otherwise a hand punch was used. Half handed to passenger and the matching half retained by conductor.

ALMEX - WHAT CAN WE DO FOR YOU?

by Ashley Bailey

A strange title indeed for an article about ticketing systems! Hopefully you will understand why a little later.

Almex, the ticketing system manufacturers, were formed in Stockholm, Sweden, during the early '50s, and went on to produce World-leading ticket machines like the Model A, Model E and Model M cancellors. An office was opened in Lewisham, then in Edenbridge, Kent, to manufacture and market the range of products for the UK bus industry.

The range of machines won Almex a huge share of the transport market, both in the UK and Worldwide. All products gained a reputation for their good audit and security features, whilst being robust and easily maintained. Almex Ticket Machines Limited of Edenbridge, went on to employ fifty staff and manufacture machines for Europe, Africa and the Far East.

The Almex mechanical products were the mainstay of business for three decades, until the 1980's, when electronic technology and the expectations of the transport industry saw a rapid decline in the demand for traditional ticket machines in the UK. The overseas market continued, but the Almex home market dwindled as electronic ticket machines became available.

During the early '80s, three rival companies were offering alternative products. These were Ticket Equipment Limited with the TIM mechanical machine and the Timtronic electronic system, and Control Systems of Uxbridge with the famous Setright and the Farespeed and Transfare range. Finally, a new company had been formed, Wayfarer, who were offering a range of electronic machines to the UK market.

At this time Almex were developing the "Model T", also known as the "Concept", their first attempt at an electronic machine for the UK market. The Model T was evaluated by Southdown in Lewes, Sussex, for a few months before it was abandoned; the technology worked well in the laboratory but failed miserably on Leyland Nationals, vibrating on cold, winter mornings. It was back to the drawing board.

Shortly after the end of the Concept, Almex became the manufacturer of electronic ticket machines (ETMs) by default. Almex took over Ticket Equipment Limited of Cirencester. The Edenbridge operation moved to the Cotswolds, and Almex now employed close to 150 staff. They had now become suppliers of the Timtronic machine, which by now had been introduced into Oxford, Devon General, Midland Red North and many other companies, including a sizable proportion of the Scottish Bus Group. Almex Ticket Equipment, the new company name, were now selling an established ETM, and the traditional mechanical products, including the TIM.

The Magnet machine followed, this was a development of Timtronic, with the major advantage of a contactless driver's modules. One of the problems seen with earlier ticket machines was the ease with which the drivers' modules could be damaged; the Magnet utilised two magnetic data transfer blocks to communicate with the ticket machine, and for collecting data from the depot. These magnets gave the machine it's name, and greatly reduced the failure rate of the ETM generally, and prevented interference with this important part of the system. The Magnet went on to be a successful, if somewhat large, ETM, and is still operating in North Western, Cheltenham and Gloucester and the Go-Ahead group, amongst others.

During 1986, Almex Ticket Equipment took over Control Systems Limited, ticket machine manufacturers who also made a very successful range of parking machines. Almex now became Almex Control Systems, and had several new products to market. These included the Control Systems Transfare, Farespeed, Farestram and the ubiquitous Setright.

Almex now had three sites in the UK; Cirencester, Uxbridge and Herne Bay. Cirencester produced the Timtronic and Magnet, and developed the future Almex products. Herne Bay produced all Control Systems products, including the parking machines. The Uxbridge site was now head office, and also held the Almex Print Division, who manufactured tickets for the full range of products.

Still essentially a Swedish-owned company Almex were now employing around 400 staff, from fifty less than four years previously. The product range included parking machines, ETMs for buses, and every possible type of leisure ticket machine.

All this time, Almex Control Systems were manufacturing excellent ticket machines for the market at that time, but were also developing a machine which was to take them through the 1990's. This machine was to be smaller, easier to use, and far more reliable than any other ETM available at the time. This machine became the A90, or Eurofare, and was installed for the first time in People's Provincial. The A90 remains the key to Almex's success today, and forms the hub of the system.

The A90 is a bus-based machine, a sister-product, the Microfare, was developed at the same time. The Microfare is a very small, hand held ticket machine capable of all the features of the A90. It allowed companies who use high-specification coaches to fit a small ticket machine on their vehicles in the smallest of cab areas, without the unit being intrusive. Whilst developed as a bus machine, the Microfare is now very popular in a wide variety of leisure applications, including golf-courses, land trains and stately homes.

In 1992 Almex won their largest single order to date, for 2,100 A90 machines for the newly united Berlin Transport. By now the UK arm of the Swedish-owned company were by far the largest division of the company. This, and a management buy-out from Almex's holding company, led to the transfer of control from Sweden to Cirencester, and the formation of the Metric Group. This new corporate name took control of Almex Transport Division, the parking division became Metric Parking. The offices in Uxbridge were closed and all administration transferred to Cirencester, with all manufacture in Herne Bay.

Almex now have several hundred sites using their range of ETMs, and literally thousands more using the Metric Groups parking machines. Success in Europe with the A90 ticket machine and the Magnetic Card cancellor has been astounding, Almex now have major customers in Germany, Spain, Italy and Sweden, and have sites in most other European countries. The old Model A still soldiers on, and has recently been supplied to Ghana, Gambia, Tanzania and Zambia.

So much for the history, onto today. The Almex A90 ticket machine can be used in conjunction with Magnetic Card Cancellors, Smart Card readers, radios, destination blinds, cash counters and most of today's on-bus technology.

The A90s tickets are large, clear, and can show the boarding and destination stage on every ticket issued. The thermal printer means that every customer can have tickets specifically designed for his company. As the tickets are so clear they tend to be read and understood by passengers.

From the driver's point of view the A90 has made life a little easier, the machines know all the fares and service details. If the driver enters the passengers destination stage, and class, the machine will produce a correctly-priced ticket. The driver does not need to remember hundreds of fares any more. As an alternative, the machine will tell a passenger how far they can travel for a set sum of money; the driver enters 50p and the tickets will be printed "Town Hall", for example.

Above all, the A90 is a driver friendly machine, which is proving to be extremely reliable in service.

The on-bus equipment forms only part of the full system; the remainder is hidden from the passengers, and can go un-noticed.

All data collected on the bus is transferred to a depot system, which allows full in-depth analysis of the information collected. Information collected in depots can be sent automatically to the company's head office by modem, if required. New fare charts and service information can also be sent from the head office to the depot by modem, greatly improving the efficiency of the ticketing system.

A bus company manager can now see, without leaving his office, if a certain driver has been running late, or whether passengers were collected from a particular stop. He will know where his passengers are getting on his buses, how much they have paid, and where they get off. He can tell from the system how much fuel his vehicles have used, and how much he needs to charge the local authority for accepting their free passes.

The real difference between Almex equipment and other options available is that Almex build machines for particular customers. Every A90 looks the same, although the way it actually operates is decided by the customer. Each company buying Almex equipment tells Almex what they want the machine to do, how they want their tickets to appear, what classes of ticket they wish to issue and so on. Almex then build the machines to suit the customer.

Recent customers for the A90 system have included Whippet Coaches, Lincolnshire RoadCar (with MCCs) and Busways, who ordered 600 units during April of this year.

These customers, as have all Almex A90 users, have gained a wealth of information from the system, and are able to use this information to improve the operation of their fleets, and therefore increase their revenue from ticket sales.

There are several possible developments for the future, Almex pride themselves on keeping abreast of technology, and building these new features into their systems. This ensures that the A90 system remains at the forefront of technology almost five years after it's inception.

Rather than telling customers what can be done with a ticketing system Almex ask what the customer wants the system to do for them. This ensures the system is always improving, with constant input from the people who have to use ticketing systems.

So, what can Almex do for you....?

DOG £00.40
From: 5 Cheltenham
To: 6 Cardiff
F0040 Rt: 100 J 1 D1234
22 Aug 94 Tck:3612 16:28
Issued subject to
Published Conditions

Dog single

RETURN
ADRET £01.40
From: 5 Cheltenham
To: 6 Cardiff
F0140 Rt: 100 J 1 D1234
22 Aug 94 Tck:3613 16:28
Issued subject to
Published Conditions

Adult return

RETURN
OAPRT £00.40
From: 8 Pembroke
To: 7 Swansea
F0040 Rt: 100 J 2 D1234
22 Aug 94 Tck:3621 16:41
Issued subject to
Published Conditions

Old Age Pensioner's return

All drawn from a Western National machine.

Almex Microfare, it's first customer trial with Whippet Coaches, during the Spring of 1989.

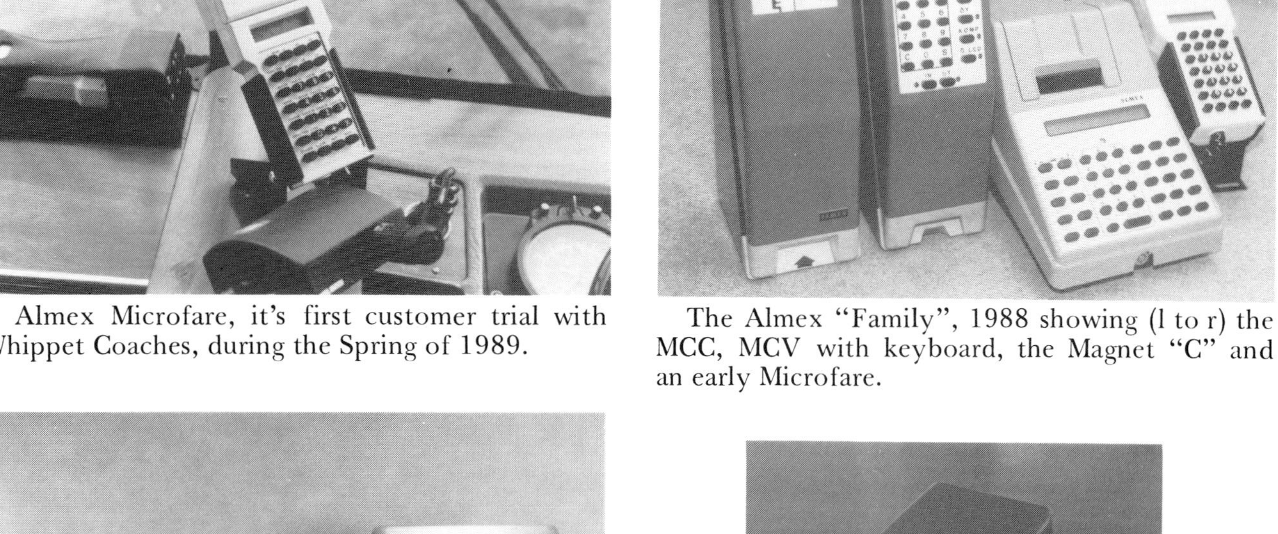

The Almex "Family", 1988 showing (l to r) the MCC, MCV with keyboard, the Magnet "C" and an early Microfare.

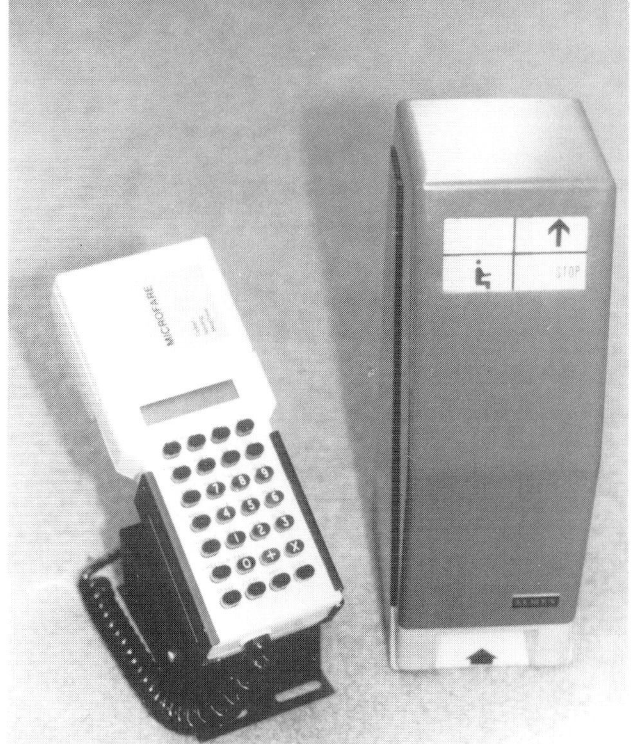

Microfare and MCC, 1989

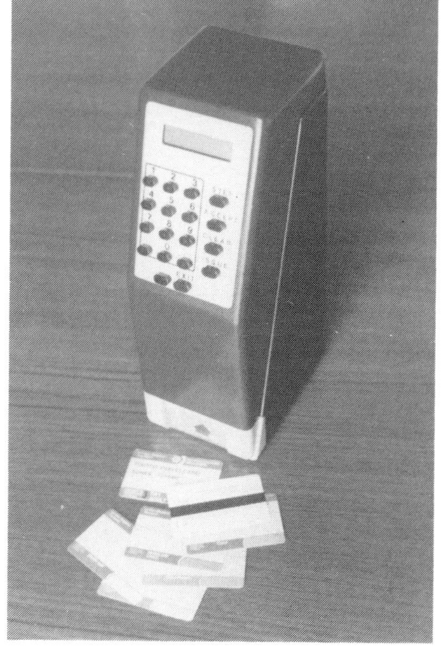

MCC - Thamesmead Trial. The Almex MCC was used by London Transport for a trial during 1988/ 1989. The machines were used to issue LT's travel-card tickets from newsagents and booking offices.

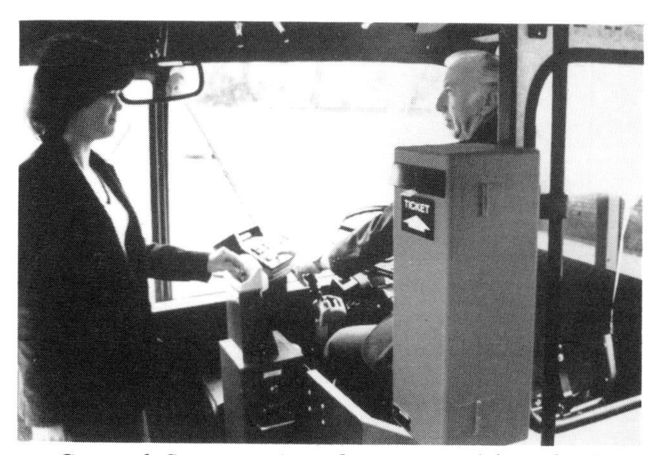

Control Systems Autofare, comprising the Key-line unit (next to driver), cash vault and remote ticket splitter. The driver checks the fare paid through a glass window in his side of the cash vault.

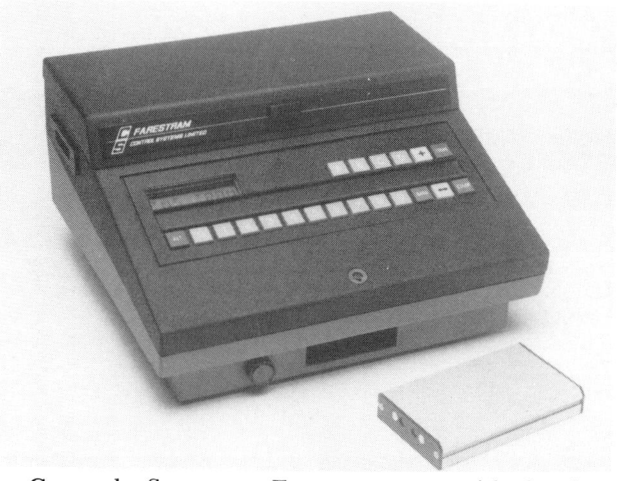

Control Systems Farestram, an ideal city-centre high speed ticket machine. The Farestram used infra-red communication between the ticket machine and the drivers module.

Lincolnshire Road Car Company Installation, showing the A90 and MCC.

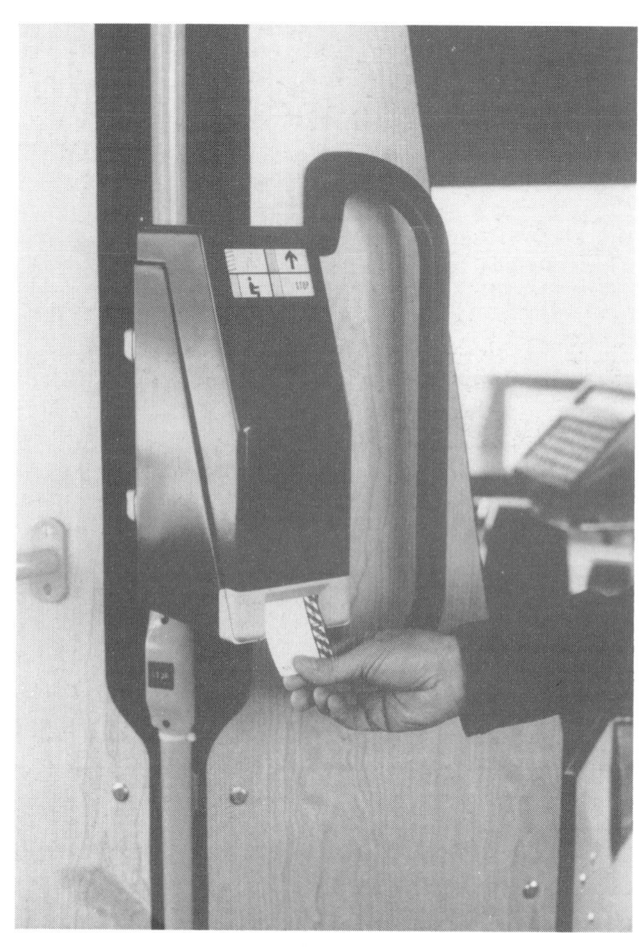

MCC in use. The MCC can carry out transactions using multi journey cards, free passes, weeklys, monthlys and passenger value cards.

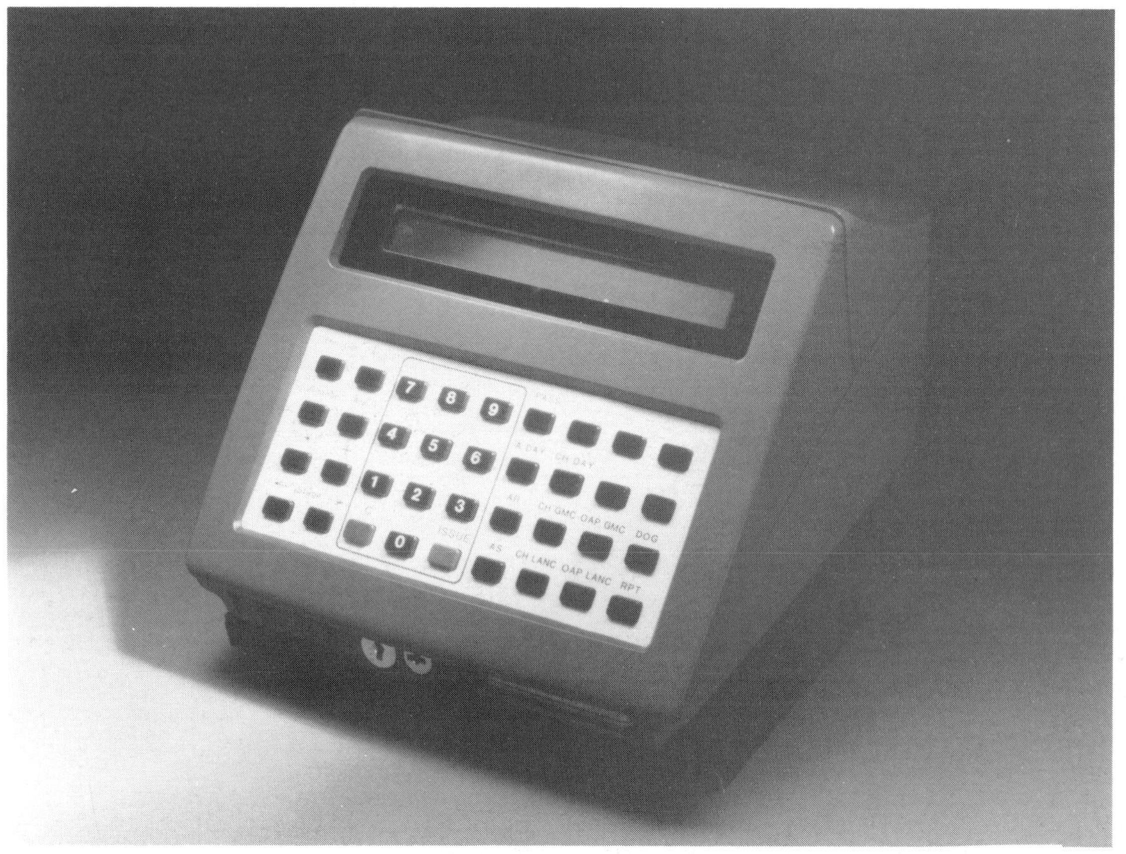

The Almex A90.

— Singing Wires - The Trolleybus —

A SILENCE OF TROLLEYBUSES

It has been claimed by those who denigrate the electric powered passenger carrying vehicles that they all look alike. Insofar as their shape makes the most efficient use of available space this is true. They do not require a massive diesel engine, but a small electric motor, they do not require fuel tanks or any paraphenalia (exhaust, gearbox etc.) associated with the use of diesel or petrol, and although their mobility is limited by the radius of their booms from the overhead wires, against this no face level pollution is caused, braking is totally efficient and the silence, especially after the day to day noises of diesels, is quite uncanny. One might also add that an efficiently built trolleybus is almost indestructable.

Three examples of "look alikes":

EF 6894 - West Hartlepool No. 34 (32-39 batch) Daimler CTM4/Metro-Vick equipment. Roe 56 seat body. In service 1938, withdrawn 1953 on closure of system (2/4/53). Jointly owned with Hartlepool Corporation. Delivered 1938 to replace single deck trolleys on the Hartlepool-West Hartlepool joint route.

AEE23 - Grimsby - Cleethorpes. (Amalgamated 1/1/57). Delivered as Grimsby No. 20 in 1946. Karrier W with Metrovick equipment. Roe 56-seat body. Withdrawn 1959-60 and sold to Bradford as No. 823, being dismantled for spares by 1962. Intended by Bradford to be rebodied by East Lancs for further service but later deleted and replaced by ex Mexborough & Swinton Sunbeam chassis. Never seen in service in Bradford.

St. Helens 387/BDJ87 (ex 187) BUT 9611T/ English Electric Equipment. East Lancs 56 seat bodies. This batch in service 1950/51 as Nos. 182-189, renumbered 382-9 in 1958 and withdrawn that year when the system closed on 31/6/58. Normally used on St. Helens - Rainhill - Prescot Loop. Fitted with safety switch to cut power if the booms splayed trying to pass under the Peasley Cross bridge if sent on this route in error as the bridge was too low for these vehicles. Sold to Bradford 1958 as Nos. 794-801 and withdrawn 1963/4. 387 - ex Bradford 799 - preserved at Sandtoft where this picture was taken.

WOLVERHAMPTON TROLLEYBUS

Routes 5 and 29 Wolverhampton-Willenhall-Walsall

by Andy Simpson and Roy Clark

To enthusiasts at least, this was probably one of Wolverhampton's best known routes, a rare example of a jointly operated trolleybus route. It had a grim industrial character all of its own summed up in the words of Robert E Jowitt in his 'A Silence of Trolleybuses' thus:

'Trolleybuses ran across scummy canals in which floated many unmentionable articles such as dead cats but no barges, and past a redundant Victorian tabernacle and some fairly antique factories, among other less noteworthy buildings . . . .'

The route had a long and distinguished transport history. Wolverhampton Tramways Co ran horse trams to Willenhall (New Road) from 6 June 1878, being taken over by Wolverhampton Corporation on 1 May 1900. Wolverhampton District Electric Tramways (WDET - part of BET Group) cars reached Deans Road from Willenhall 4 November 1902; the Wolverhampton Horse cars running to Deans Road to meet the electric cars from 24 January 1903, until 24 January 1904. The route then closed for conversion to the electric Lorain surface contact system, which was used by Wolverhampton in preference to 'unsightly' overhead wires. Several Lorain studs reclaimed from Wolverhampton's Cleveland Rd Depot can be seen relaid at The National Tramway Museum, Crich, plus one sectioned at the Science Museum, South Kensington.

It was Wolverhampton's last horse tram route. Wolverhampton Lorain cars commenced running to Coventry Street 2 April 1904 and were extended the quarter mile to the then borough boundary at Deans Road 23 April 1904, passengers having to change at the boundary for WDET cars to Willenhall and beyond until through running over WDET tracks commenced 18 April 1906 using dual-equipped single deck Corporation trams, the WDET cars being cut back to Willenhall Market Place and running on to Bilston and Darlaston. Walsall Corporation trams also ran to Willenhall from July 1905 over WDET tracks. This became Wolverhampton Corporation's route six, the through fare in 1914 being 2½d. Single deck cars had to be used due to the low railway bridge at Horseley Fields.

Wolverhampton Corporation converted its Willenhall route to overhead operation 22 July 1921, and in March 1922 took delivery of its last new trams, Brush built single-deck 'Tividale' lookalikes Nos. 62-69 which were used extensively on the route, but only until 8 August 1926 when motor-buses replaced the trams. The conversion to overhead operation had of course removed the need for the change to/from the Lorain system at Deans Road, where as recently as October 1992 roadworks revealed tram track still in situ.

Around 1922 there had been the first suggestion of a through service by Walsall trams to Wolverhampton. This was not followed up, possibly due to the low LNWR bridge at Horseley Fields. Wolverhampton purchased the Deans Road-Willenhall section from WDET 9 August 1926, having finished the tram service the previous night; after track removal and overhead reconstruction Wolverhampton began running Dodson bodied Tilling-Stevens TS6 single deck trolleybuses from Horseley Fields to Neachells Lane 16 May 1927, being extended to Willenhall 16 September 1927, with a turning circle at the Market Place. Walsall continued to run trams to Willenhall until 3 February 1929 and then replaced them with motorbuses, a trial joint motorbus service commencing between the two towns the next day, this being the first ever through service on the route. This venture was so successful that it was decided to convert the whole route to trolleybus operation.

Double deck trolleybuses began running from Walsall to Willenhall 22 July 1931. These four vehicles, AEC 663T's 151/2 and Guy BTX 153/4 were Walsall's first trolleybuses. The low bridge at Horseley Fields was altered to allow double-deck operation, the joint Walsall-Wolverhampton service commencing Monday 16 November 1931. This was the culmination of the plans of both towns to operate a through trolleybus service put forward in their respective 1925 bills.

The resulting route was six miles long, running initially from Horseley Fields, Wolverhampton but later altered to a loop around St. James' Square. The route then ran via the Willenhall Road and Willenhall (High Street) - New Road - Walsall Road -Walsall (Town End). The service terminated in Wolverhampton Street until Town End Street was wired in 1955. At Willenhall there was a junction with Wolverhampton's trolleybus route number 25 to Bilston and Fighting Cocks from 27 October 1930 until this route closed Sunday 25 October 1964. The 90 degree cross-over which formed part of the 'spider's web' at Willenhall was salvaged by Roy Clark, for eventual use at the Black Country Museum.

Likely passengers on this route, in addition to shoppers travelling to/from the markets of the three towns on the route would be school children, and workers at the Chillington Tool Co., Gaunt & Hickman, John Hills & Sons and Qualcast Ltd. There were section pillars at half mile intervals, permitting sections of wiring to be isolated if damaged. On the Wolverhampton side they were located at Five Ways, Shakespeare Street, and Minerva Lane. Pillar with automatic sectioning switch next, then at Haywards; Merry Boys; Deans Road (with connection to rectifier sub-station); Noose Lane, Summer Street; Willenhall; Willenhall Station (junction with 25 route). The Portobello-Cleveland Road stretch of the route was dead straight and duly became the fastest section on the system, known to crews as the 'Mad Mile'.

From St. James' Square a depot connection joined the route to the Bilston/Darlaston route, via Piper's Row and Bilston Street.

Fare stages on the route were: Walsall-Wolverhampton; Town End Bank; Manor Road; Lane Avenue; Bloxwich Lane; Bentley Mill Lane; Bentley; Bentley Cemetery; Crescent Road; Willenhall; New Street; Nechells Lane, Hurstbourne Crescent; East Parkway; St Matthews Church; St James' Square. From Wolverhampton to Willenhall, speed limits were 30 mph except for the following: 20mph; High St., Portobello between Brikkiln St., and School St. 15 mph; In Lower Horseley Fields when passing over the canal bridge and under the railway bridge. There were the usual restrictions over junctions and crossings, limiting speed to 8 mph at these points.

By the second world war period Wolverhampton's route numbers were 5 to Willenhall, 5A to Walsall, changing by the 1950's to 5 to Willenhall, 29 to Walsall (then sharing the same route number as Walsall used). Outwards from Wolverhampton the WCT trolleybuses showed 'Walsall via Willenhall' but they showed merely 'Wolverhampton' if bound from Walsall. The Walsall short workings to Willinehall showed route no. 28. F W York (Buses Illustrated Jan. 1967) remembers wartime bomb damage on the route with journeys interrupted by passengers having to dismount and walk round the bomb crater blocking the road to board another vehicle waiting on the other side of the obstruction with battery turns being made into side streets.

The route gave steady, unspectacular service until the 1960's. In March 1961 Wolverhampton Council's trolleybus abandonment programme stated that the joint route to Walsall would be the last to be converted. Maintenance continued - by December 1962 Wolverhampton had fitted new twin-line hangers with steel spacer bars (UK Patent No. 537899). Twenty-eight of this type of hanger were obtained by Roy Clark and have been utilised in the museum's trolleybus route (along the double-line section).

By 1962 it was anticipated that the route would survive as Wolverhampton's last route to circa 1968, but closure was brought forward by the disruptive effects of the construction of the M6 motorway, which was planned to cross the 29 route at Bentley. Rumours that Walsall might take over the whole route proved to be unfounded. An early interruption to service came on 14 May 1963 when power failures affected routes 5/29 and 2/7 (Whitmore Reans, Darlaston). There was a second failure early in 1965. Traction poles on the Walsall side of the route were repainted in August 1964.

The end was, by now, inevitable - operation ceased earlier than expected since construction of the motorway required a bridge to carry the Walsall-Wolverhampton road over the motorway. There had been an agreement between Wolverhampton and Walsall that the through trolleybus service would continue until 1967 but conversion was brought forward by the engineering works. Walsall's first trolleybus route thus became its first trolleybus abandonment. It was not thought advisable to operate trolleybuses over the approaches to the motorway, and this, coupled with Wolverhampton's rapidly accelerating conversion programme signalled the end, which came on 31 October 1965.

When it was decided to abandon the route in 1965, Walsall received £15,000 compensation from the Ministry of Transport since their motorway construction had prompted the abandonment earlier than expected. Walsall used the money to purchase 8 replacement motor buses.

The last service Wolverhampton vehicle on the 29 route on the night of 31 October 1965 was 434, followed by 446 hired specially by the NTA (National Trolleybus Association, now part of the Trolleybus Museum Co.) (446 was also the last trolleybus to Wednesfield in 1963 and to Dudley in March 1967! It was retained for possible preservation until scrapped September 1968.) This special run, after the last service bus, left Cleveland Road depot at 23.05 for St James' Square running hence to Willenhall and Walsall, and was not widely advertised. Roy Clark witnessed the last service bus to Willenhall, Wolverhampton 432. The last Walsall vehicle on the route was 343 on the 23.04 ex Wolverhampton.

A number of Wolverhampton vehicles were withdrawn upon the closure of the route, leaving just 30 trolleybuses in stock to operate the Dudley route (reduced to 23 and no spares by the end in March 1967).

Wolverhampton vehicles withdrawn 31/10/65 were as follows:

Park-Royal bodied 1948 Sunbeam F4 478 - the last 8 foot wide vehicle to run in the Wolverhampton fleet. To the surprise of the enthusiast fraternity, since Wolverhampton withdrew the Park-Royal bodied vehicles first instead of the Roe re-bodied examples which were in better condition, 478 had her rear end rebuilt in early 1965 and was repainted that May. Despite this she went into store at Park Lane Garage 25/10/65 where she lingered until passing to Walsall breaker Gammell by February 1967, having first donated her motor to 1948 Sunbeam W 451 in late 1966.

1945 Sunbeam W's 408/9 to Park Lane on the morning of 31st October; to Gammell c. December 1965.

1945 Sunbeam W's 411/13 - initially to Ferromet (breakers) but thence to Gammell Nov. 65. Sunbeam W's 418 (1945) and 420 (1946) - to Park Lane on the morning of the final day; hence to Gammell December 1965.

1946 Sunbeam W's 421/3 went initially to Ferromet and thence to Gammell Nov 65. Similar vehicle 422 went to Park Lane on the last morning and hence to Gammell Dec 65; 1946 Sunbeam W 428, latterly used as a driver training vehicle, went initially to Ferromet and hence to Gammell.

Ferromet also acquired at the same time the chassis of 1947 Sunbeam W 445, withdrawn Jan 65 and later stripped for spares, and the accident damaged 1945 Sunbeam W 415 that had been damaged 24/8/65 whilst running on the joint route.

Walsall did not immediately withdraw any trolleybuses although 1946 Sunbeam W's 234-

237 were withdrawn 31/12/65. Conversion to motorbuses meant the closure of the Deans Road rectifier on the electrical distribution system, the overhead being disconnected at feeder pillars within a day. Some of the overhead was rapidly demolished within a few days on the section covered by motorway construction. The Willenhall turning circle had been removed by 4 November 1965. In Walsall, the former joint route wires at Townend Bank were not severed and tied off until November 1966. In March 1967 Walsall removed remaining wires in Walsall Road, Willenhall, completing the removal of overhead on the Wolverhampton side of the M6, after which the wires on the Walsall side of the M6 remained intact until demolished mid December 1968, due to construction of the Wolverhampton Road new dual carriageway; traction pole removal on the route commenced c. March 1970, prompted by a fatal accident when a taxi collided with a redundant pole. Even then a short length of wiring remained for feeder purposes from the town centre to the Blue Lane sub-station until finally removed on Sunday 26 April 1970, covering the Canal Street-Town End Street section. Most redundant poles on Wolverhampton's Willenhall section were removed from the Willenhall end from November 1967. Remaining poles served as lighting standards until replaced by new standards c. March 1972. Wolverhampton had completed demolition of the Willenhall section wiring by late May 1966. Some items were reclaimed for re-use on the Dudley route. In February 1988 five poles remained on the Wolverhampton side of the motorway, three in Willenhall Road close together - one opposite pair and a singleton, of which the singleton had gone by 1989; one at Portobello by the railway bridge, still extant in 1994 and one on private property in Willenhall that still retained long lengths of span wire complete with insulators. At least two poles remained in St. James' Square until 1983. With completion of the Wolverhampton Ring Road, St. James' Square itself has largely been demolished.

Upon conversion the route remained jointly operated until the formation of WMPTE in 1969, the replacement motorbuses taking 28 minutes for the run as had the trolleybuses. The Walsall terminus was moved a few yards to Shaw St.

Vehicle Notes:

Local enthusiast Deryck Vernon has kindly provided sightings of single deckers on the route and Bournemouth vehicles; (Wolverhampton borrowed a dozen Bournemouth Sunbeam MS2 trolleybuses from 1940-1948). 1934-6 Sunbeam single decks 207 29/9/45* 208 3/9/47; 209 20/3/46; 233 29/9/56* B161 2/12/44*; B168 28/11/47. (*These dates were Saturdays-Service extras after matches at Molineux). Circa 1961, Wolverhampton's contribution was normally 1949 Guy/BTH and Sunbeam vehicles. Walsall's ten 1951 Sunbeam F4A's Nos. 334-343, were used when new on the joint service, and were the most silent and smooth running trolleybuses ever used in Walsall. The ex-Hastings W's, Nos. 303-310, purchased in 1959 replaced the F4's on the joint route; they were unpopular since cramped, but fast running. No wonder the Walsall crews called them 'Sardine Cans' on their runs to 'Hampton'. They were in turn replaced in 1962 by the eight ex-Ipswich Sunbeam F4's, Nos. 345-8/351-4 with their distinctive arrangement of the 'Wolverhampton' diagonal in their small destination box. The Hastings vehicles did appear from time to time until the route closed. A photograph is known of Walsall 306 on the 29 route taken on 12 May 1961.

On Saturday 21/7/62 on the 29 route to Walsall were Wolverhampton 431 and Walsall 346 (ex-Ipswich 125). On 6 July 1964, Wolverhampton 449 was on the joint service (Buses Illustrated, Jan 1967). On 26 June 1965, Walsall (ex-Ipswich) 354 turned over at the Walsall side of Bentley on a run to Wolverhampton when a pedestrian was killed and 12 passengers injured; an earlier accident on the route involved Wolverhampton Guy BT 648 on 15/11/62, the vehicle being withdrawn and passing to Everall in March 1963, and thence to Smith, Coseley Road, Bilston for scrap.

To replace the 25 route trolleybuses, in October 1964 Wolverhampton borrowed, and then in December 1964 purchased 1949 built Birmingham Corporation Daimler CVD6's 1935/52/98/9, 2000/1-4/7/23, with Metro-Cammell H54R bodies. They were stored when the 147-156 batch of Guy Arab Vs were delivered, but were used from 1/11/65 to replace the trolleys on the 5/29, Nine being relicensed and two (2003/4) being broken up for spares. Survivors of this batch - 1935/52, 98-9, 2002/7/23 were not withdrawn until February 1967.

The Walsall route was host to several enthusiast tours in the 1960s.

On Sunday 11th June 1961 the Tramway Museum Society ran their first 'Trackless' tour, starting with a tour of the Walsall system, with 873, then changing to Sunbeam F4A 870, with its distinctive 'goldfish bowl' bodywork to run over part of the route to Willenhall, hence to Bilston and Fighting Cocks - the first Walsall trolleybus to run on these Wolverhampton routes - and then to Cleveland Road Depot and back to Walsall.

On Sunday 22nd September 1963, 55 members of the Wolverhampton Trolleybus Group (precursor of the present Black Country Museum Transport Group), plus Walsall manager Edgley Cox (who sadly passed away in January 1994) used 'Goldfish bowl' 869 as the first Walsall trolleybus to reach the centre of Wolverhampton on a Walsall-Willenhall - Bilston - Fighting Cocks - Dudley - Wolverhampton - Merry Hill - Walsall grand tour, making 869 the first Walsall trolleybus to reach Worcestershire when it ran to Dudley. The tour returned to Walsall via the joint route.

Early in 1964 the NTA used Wolverhampton's 1945 Sunbeam W 408 to cover the joint route and the rest of Wolverhampton's remaining wiring, and on 11th April 1965 the same organisation used Wolverhampton's most recently repainted trolleybus, the rebodied Sunbeam 455, to cover that town's remaining wiring on a Walsall-Whitmore Reans-Darlaston-Dudley tour, carrying about 30 NTA members.

This just left the NTA special on the last night, as recorded earlier in this account.

A handful of trolleybuses survive which may have run on the route.

Of the eight ex-Ipswich vehicles that were so much a feature of the route from 1962, one - Walsall 347, is now restored to its original condition as Ipswich 126 and is part of the extensive Ipswich Transport Museum collection.

The two Walsall Sunbeam F4As that ran enthusiasts' tours of the route, 869 and 870, are long scrapped, but three of their sister vehicles survive - 862 in working order at the Black Country Museum, 864 as a store shed at Sandtoft Trolleybus Museum, and 872 at the Aston Manor Road Transport Museum, Witton, Birmingham, where it is on loan from Sandtoft.

Four Wolverhampton trolleybuses survive, and all four are likely to have run on the Walsall route.

Perhaps the rarest survivor is 1931 Guy BTX 78, in unrestored condition at the Black Country Museum, Dudley having been rescued from use as a farm store in Southern Ireland in July 1990. Two of Wolverhampton's typical Park Royal bodied vehicles survive both in unrestored state following external store in the 1960s/70s; 1949 Sunbeam F4 616 is at the North West Museum of Transport, St Helens; Guy BT 654, the last Guy trolleybus built in 1950 is stored by the Trolleybus Museum Co. in Northants.

The only operational Wolverhampton trolleybus is currently 1946 Sunbeam W 433, rebodied by Roe in 1959 and running most Sundays at the Black Country Museum.

Several fellow members of the Black Country Museum Transport Group have contributed details of this article; Group members help to restore, operate and maintain trams and trolleybuses at the Museum's open-air site in Dudley with its operating tram and trolleybus route crossing the site, and receive a regular news letter. Details (sae please) from 122 Coniston Road, Wolverhampton, West Midlands WV6 9DU.

SERVICE 5 — **WOLVERHAMPTON—WILLENHALL** — **TROLLEY BUS SERVICE**

MONDAY TO FRIDAY

			AM	AM	AM	AM	AM	AM	AM		PM		PM		
Wolverhampton	St. James Square	dep.	6 25	6 40	6 48	7 20	8 12	8 43	8 54	every	7 14	every	1058	....	....
Willenhall	Dale Cinema	arr.	6 39	6 54	7 2	7 34	8 26	8 57	9 8	16 mins.	7 28	32 mins.	1112	....	....

			AM	AM	AM	AM	AM	AM	AM		PM		PM		
Willenhall	Dale Cinema	dep.	6 40	6 55	7 2	7 34	8 26	8 57	9 8	every	7 28	every	1112	....	....
Wolverhampton	St. James Square	arr.	6 54	7 9	7 16	7 48	8 40	8 11	9 22	16 mins.	7 42	32 mins.	1126	....	....

SATURDAY

			AM	AM		PM										
Wolverhampton	St. James Square	dep.	6 42	9 20	every	6 42	....	....	....	....	....	....	....	....	....	....
Willenhall	Dale Cinema	arr.	6 56	9 34	16 mins.	6 56	....	....	....	....	....	....	....	....	....	....

			AM	AM		PM										
Willenhall	Dale Cinema	dep.	6 56	9 34	every	6 56	....	....	....	....	....	....	....	....	....	....
Wolverhampton	St. James Square	arr.	7 10	9 48	16 mins.	7 10	....	....	....	....	....	....	....	....	....	....

SUNDAY

			PM				PM		PM		PM		PM		PM
Wolverhampton	St. James Square	dep.	3 28	....	every	....	8 53	....	9 15	....	9 47	....	1017	....	1048
Willenhall	Dale Cinema	arr.	3 42	....	10 minutes approx.	....	9 7	....	9 29	....	10 1	....	1031	....	11 2

			PM				PM		PM		PM		PM		PM
Willenhall	Dale Cinema	dep.	3 42	....	Every	....	9 9	....	9 29	....	10 1	....	1032	....	11 2
Wolverhampton	St. James Square	arr.	3 56	....	10 minutes approx.	....	9 23	....	9 43	....	1015	....	1046	....	1116

For additional service, see Wolverhampton—Willenhall—Walsall Service No. 29.

SERVICE 29 — **WOLVERHAMPTON—WILLENHALL—WALSALL** — **TROLLEY BUS SERVICE**

Operated jointly with Walsall Corporation Transport Department

MONDAY TO FRIDAY

			AM	AM	AM	AM	AM	AM	AM	AM		AM		PM	
Wolverhampton	St. James Square	dep.	5 0	5 30	5 45	6 0	6 15	6 31	6 47	6 50	every	8 50	every	3 38	every
Willenhall	Dale Cinema	"	5 14	5 44	5 59	6 14	6 29	6 45	7 1	7 4	4	9 4	8	3 52	4
Walsall	Townend Bank	arr.	5 28	5 58	6 13	6 28	6 43	6 59	7 15	7 18	minutes	9 18	minutes	4 6	minutes

			AM	AM		AM	AM	AM	AM		AM		PM	
Walsall	Townend Bank	dep.	4 56	5 30	every	6 30	6 42	6 45	6 50	every	8 50	every	3 38	every
Willenhall	Dale Cinema	"	5 10	5 44	15	6 44	6 56	6 59	7 4	4	9 4	8	3 52	4
Wolverhampton	St. James Square	arr.	5 24	5 58	minutes	6 58	7 10	7 13	7 18	minutes	9 18	minutes	4 6	minutes

			PM	PM	PM	PM	PM	PM		PM	PM						
Wolverhampton	St. James Square	dep.	6 38	6 46	6 54	7 2	7 6	7 10	every	1054	11 0	....	....	....	....	....	....
Willenhall	Dale Cinema	"	6 52	7 0	7 8	7 16	7 20	7 24	8	11 8	1114	....	....	....	....	....	....
Walsall	Townend Bank	arr.	7 6	7 14	7 22	7 30	7 34	7 38	minutes	1122	1128	....	....	....	....	....	....

			PM	PM	PM	PM	PM	PM		PM	PM						
Walsall	Townend Bank	dep.	6 38	6 46	6 54	7 2	7 6	7 10	every	1054	11 0	....	....	....	....	....	....
Willenhall	Dale Cinema	"	6 52	7 0	7 8	7 16	7 20	7 24	8	11 8	1114	....	....	....	....	....	....
Wolverhampton	St. James Square	arr.	7 6	7 14	7 22	7 30	7 34	7 38	minutes	1122	1128	....	....	....	....	....	....

SATURDAY

			AM	AM	AM	AM	AM	AM	AM	AM	AM	AM	AM	AM		AM	
Wolverhampton	St. James Square	dep.	5 0	....	5 30	5 45	....	6 0	6 15	6 24	6 30	6 36	6 45	6 54	every	9 0	....
Willenhall	Dale Cinema	"	5 14	5 14	5 44	5 59	5 59	6 14	6 29	6 38	6 44	6 50	6 59	7 8	6	9 14	....
Walsall	Townend Bank	arr.	....	5 28	5 58	....	6 13	6 28	6 43	6 52	6 58	7 4	7 13	7 22	minutes	9 28	....

			AM	AM	AM	AM	AM	AM	AM	AM	AM	AM	AM	AM		AM	
Walsall	Townend Bank	dep.	5 0	....	5 30	5 45	....	6 0	6 15	6 24	6 30	6 36	6 45	6 54	every	9 0	....
Willenhall	Dale Cinema	"	5 14	5 14	5 44	5 59	5 59	6 14	6 29	6 38	6 44	6 50	6 59	7 8	6	9 14	....
Wolverhampton	St. James Square	arr.	....	5 28	5 58	....	6 13	6 28	6 43	6 52	6 58	7 4	7 13	7 22	minutes	9 28	....

Continued on next page

1959

EXAMPLES OF WALSALL AND WOLVERHAMPTON VEHICLES

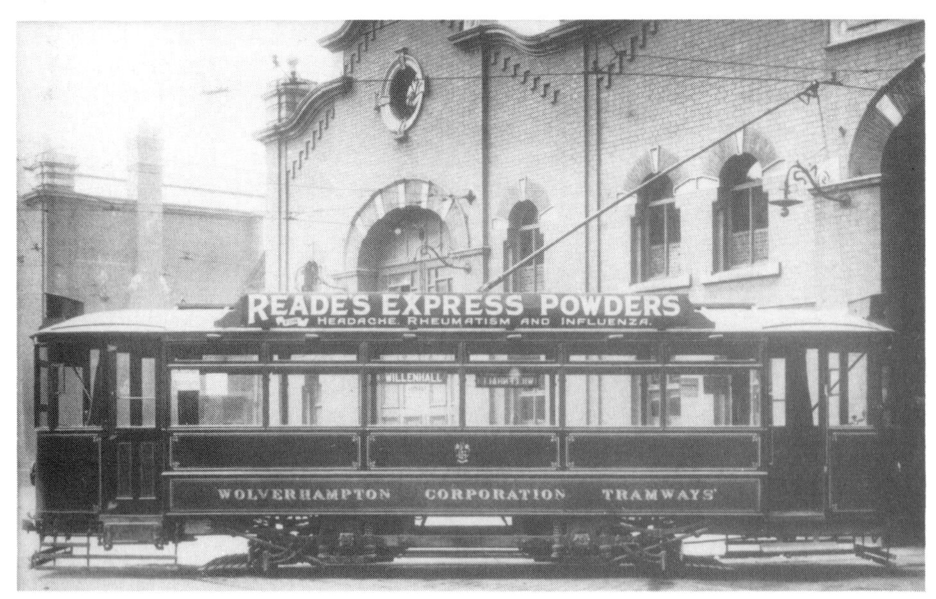

Wolverhampton's last new tram, 1922 Brush built car No. 69 poses outside Cleveland Road Depot. The design is clearly based on the ten 'Tividale' type cars supplied by Brush to the Birmingham and Midland Tramways Joint Committee in 1919. No.s 62-9 had BTH motors, Dick Kerr controllers and Brush-built Peckham Pendulum P-22 trucks. [Tramway & Railway World]

Last Wolverhampton normal service vehicle on the last night of the joint route was 1947 Sunbeam W 434, rebodied by Roe. It is seen here in happier times in Stafford Street on the Low Hill-Merry Hill cross town route, and joined the dwindling number of trolleybuses on Wolverhampton's last trolleybus route to Dudley until withdrawn in January 1967 when it was stripped for spares. [W.J. Haynes]

Classic Park-Royal bodied Sunbeam F4 Wolverhampton 626 is seen here at St. James' Square, hotly persued by sister vehicle 622. Delivered in 1950, No. 626 lasted until withdrawal of the Whitmore Reans-Bilston-Darlaston route in August 1965, the conversion which preceded that of the Walsall joint route. [W.J. Haynes]

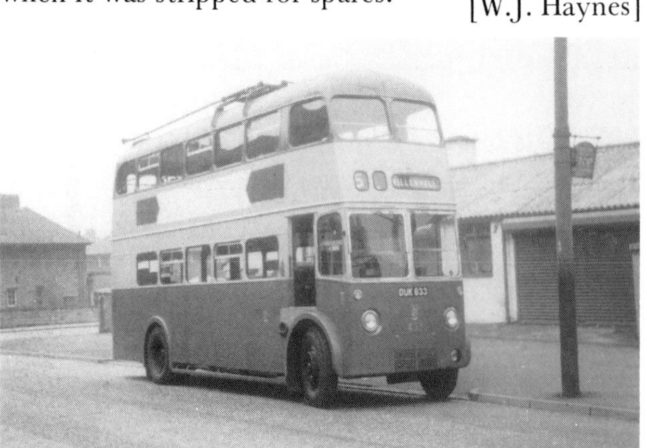

Now Wolverhampton's sole operating trolleybus survivor, 1946 Sunbeam W No. 433 pauses in St. James Square. It was rebodied by Roe in 1959 and ran until closure of Wolverhampton's last trolleybus route to Dudley in March 1967. [A. Simpson Collection]

Last operating survivor of Wolverhampton's 1949 batch of Guy BT's, 482-499, was 498, seen here pulling away from St. James' Square prior to its withdrawal upon conversion of the Whitmore Reans-Bilston-Darlaston route in August 1965. [A. Simpson Collection]

Ex Hastings 'Sardine Can' BDY 812, now Walsall 306, sets off for Wolverhampton. Delivered to the sea-side in 1948, it entered Walsall service 1.10.59 and fell victim to the purge of ex-Walsall secondhand trolleys in February 1970.

[C.W. Routh]

GFU 694 Grimsby-Cleethorpes 161. Delivered 1950 as Cleethorpes 61. BUT 9611T chassis with Metrovick equipment and a NCB built body seating 54. Withdrawn 1960 and sold to Walsall with the remainder of the batch 159-162. Rebuilt by Walsall with a lengthened chassis and body, the rear entrance being replaced with a forward door. This hybrid, seating 69, entered Walsall service after a three year delay on 15 July 1962, but was withdrawn 16 September 1970.

After the joint route conversion Wolverhampton and Walsall continued motor bus operation. This scene at the Walsall Terminus c. 1965-1969 captures Walsall's 1961 AEC Regent V No. 900 awaiting departure to Wolverhampton whilst Sunbeam F4A 869 - which had itself run to Wolverhampton in 1963 - passes behind. No. 900 was withdrawn in 1972 by WMPTE and went to Machines & Plant Exporting of Bromley in December 1973.

[R.F. Mack]

Just off from St. James' Square for yet another run to Walsall is Wolverhampton's Roe-bodied Sunbeam W 418, withdrawn on closure of the joint route and meeting its maker courtesy of Walsall breaker Gammell.

[R.F. Mack]

Town End Bank is the setting for Walsall 343, a 1951 Sunbeam F4 with Brush bodywork withdrawn in 1966.

[C. Carter]

PLAXTON FORD. R 192

PLAXTONS put quality coach-building on to today's newest chassis. Ford advanced engineering design and PLAXTON superb Embassy and Panorama coachwork combine to give you outstanding comfort, styling and performance in the FORD R 192. Be distinctive, specify PLAXTONS today's finest luxury coaches.

PANORAMA I

The Panorama body was first named in 1958, when a prototype was built to the design of Ben Goodfellow, the Sheffield United Tours General Manager. At the British Coach Rally that year their No. 286 appeared, bearing the name 'Panorama Pioneer'. There have, of course, been other vehicles with panoramic glazing, and some of those built in the 1930s were as much an advance then as the Plaxton body was in 1958. Within a few years the Panorama body was to take on a life of its own, gradually losing all the styling elements of its predecessors. The main advertisement above dates back to July 1966 - the use by a parts supplier of the same drawing is ingenious. The drawing opposite is of a 1963 model and the photograph of a 'pure' 1967 Panorama I on a Daimler Roadliner chassis. It has been claimed with some justification that this style was the finest produced.

[Photo - Vintage Roadscene Publications Ltd.]

THE NEW PLAXTONS

SUPERB COACHES RALLY PROVED WITH A HOST OF SPARKLING NEW FEATURES

THE NEW PANORAMA

THE NEW PANORAMA

More improvements to the amazing Panorama—now surely today's most advanced luxury coach. The new stainless steel side mouldings reduce cleaning time for the operator. New zone toughened windscreen (interchangeable with the rear screen) means increased safety for driver and passenger. New luxury seats, deeper side windows and individual ventilation promise extra relaxing vision and comfort for today's particular passengers.

— The Vehicle We Ride In —

FLICKER FLASHBACK

December 1913 and a new Daimler stands ready for use. The chassis is of the "CC" model designation fitted with K.P. Knight's famous "Silent Knight" 4-cylinder sleeve valve engine developing (nominally) 40 h.p. The gearbox is chain-driven - to add to the cacophony of solid tyres on cobbles - but final drive is by shaft. Brakes were unassisted mechanical, speed 12 mph officially but according to a road test 19 maximum. We do not know the body builder but the seating reflects tram thinking, and the drop window at the rear utilizes pure railway design with a perforated leather strap engaging on a peg. To lower, one pulled the strap towards one and used a suitable hole for the correct level of ventilation. Five headlights, one tishy tail light but the few in the interior probably taxed the batteries output. Quite a delightful gem.

Photographed at Cook Street Gate, Coventry.

TS3 of 1915 with Dodson bodywork for
Walsall Corporation.

TS7 of 1929 for Thomas Tilling with
home-produced bodywork.

From the grim necessity of War to the smooth luxury of Peace...

Back again to PASSENGER TRANSPORT

After nearly six years of complete war work, Tilling-Stevens are putting into production those plans for modern public transport vehicles which have hitherto been just a drawing-board ideal.

Soon the new Tilling-Stevens buses and coaches will make their bow to a comfort-hungry public.

TILLING-STEVENS
LIMITED MAIDSTONE
Telephone
MAIDSTONE 3327

BUILDERS OF
MODERN PASSENGER TRANSPORT VEHICLES

1921

This Tilling-Stevens bus was the first in its class

Shortly we will announce our

1947
RANGE

DEVELOPED AFTER CONSULTATION WITH MANY LEADING PASSENGER TRANSPORT OPERATORS

TILLING-STEVENS LTD
VICTORIA WORKS • MAIDSTONE

PRECISION BUILT *for* LONG DISTANCE

An ever increasing number of people want to visit the Continent and they want to travel in comfort and with confidence.

For Continental road travel the right vehicle is essential. Many years of experience and research are the reasons why Tilling-Stevens buses and coaches have proved to be so suitable for long distance touring. Being precision built they combine the greatest reliability with the utmost of comfort and luxury.

That is why the Tilling-Stevens coach (illustrated above) is being used for tours to the Mediterranean Coast.

TILLING-STEVENS
LIMITED
MAIDSTONE

It is hard to know what the real epitaph for Tillings-Stevens should be. The first vehicles of 1911 represented the brains of W.A. Stevens coupled to the buying power of Thomas Tilling (the bus operator) who was in need of a vehicle which could be driven by non-mechanically minded men, to whom a gear box was an alien organism. The elimination of the gearbox also meant that tram drivers could easily be converted from electrical 'stepless' driving to a similar mechanical arrangement. Basically what Stevens achieved was to marry an electric motor to a normal petrol engine and generator and persuade them to move a bus. The vehicles were slow, but steady and suffered little in the way of mechanical problems.

But that was a long, long time before these advertisements and, indeed, after Tillings parted company with their offspring in 1931, the firm became T.S. Motors Ltd and to all intents and purposes had faded from the main-line bus scene by the outbreak of war, despite buying up another bus chassis building 'name', Vulcan from Southport in 1937. Building wartime petrol-electric searchlight generating sets put them financially back on their feet but their postwar attempt to return to coach and bus building fizzled out, leaving us with, at least, a legacy of lost dreams.

Reliability
on the road
VM 1950

THE BIG (BEAUTIFUL) BEDFORD

In 1956 when "Rosie" (972 ANK) fleet No.1 with ESJ Motors of Saltash was delivered her official price was shown as either £3,190 with a 115 h.p. six-cylinder Bedford petrol engine or £3,577 with a 102 h.p. Perkins R6 diesel. This price which was bought 'out of season' was 'ex coachworks' and did not include the cost of delivering the chassis to the coachbuilders' works. The diesel price included the vital necessary extra sound insulation and one could buy as optional extras a mechanical tyre pump at £10.50 plus Purchase Tax (a forbear of V.A.T.) of £2.62½ (i.e. 25%) or an Eaton 2-speed axle (economy at the cost of complication, especially with a none-too-careful driver) at £174 + P.T. £43.50.

But August 1956 saw, for the first time, the availability of power steering. At a stroke not only could men drive coaches with consummate ease but women could take over. That was the theory but the unassisted clutch was still heavy, the gearbox only had synchromesh on the top three (of four) and the brakes - massive drums with (in theory) nearly 500 sq.ft. of lining area - were only assisted by a single servo and really still relied on a strong right ankle and size 12 boot. Some ladies did drive them and indeed the introduction of power steering brought Bedford design forward with a gigantic leap.

Bedford thought so as well and pushed it hard. Oddly no price was quoted . . .

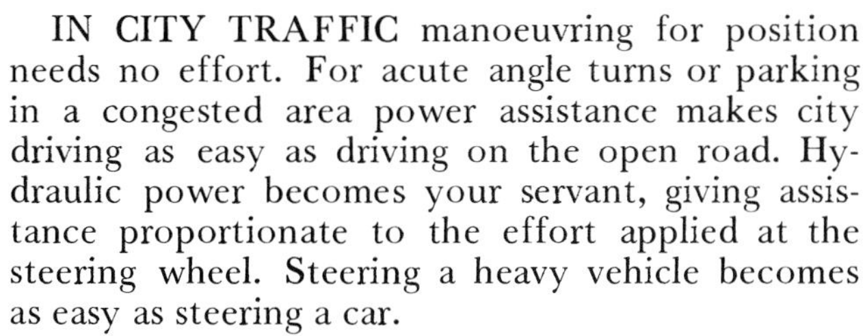

IN CITY TRAFFIC manoeuvring for position needs no effort. For acute angle turns or parking in a congested area power assistance makes city driving as easy as driving on the open road. Hydraulic power becomes your servant, giving assistance proportionate to the effort applied at the steering wheel. Steering a heavy vehicle becomes as easy as steering a car.

ON WINDING ROADS power-assisted steering reduces driving fatigue, promotes greater safety and faster schedules. Steering responds instantly to a touch of the wheel. Turns are made quicker, safer and with the utmost facility. Think what this means in terms of driver confidence. Drivers remain physically fresh and mentally alert throughout the whole distance.

ON BAD ROAD SURFACES power-assisted steering ensures positive control by eliminating wheel kick. Road shocks are not passed back to the steering wheel. The power which multiplies the pull applied to the steering wheel works "in reverse" to reduce wheel kick by the inverse ratio. The tendency for front wheels to be deflected by obstacles is resisted by power assistance.

IN THE GARAGE power comes to your assistance when parking the vehicle in a tight corner. With power-assisted steering front wheels can easily be swung from lock to lock without heavy manual effort or strain on the steering gear, even when creeping slowly into position. At all times the power assistance is a well-disciplined servant – responsive, safe and absolutely reliable.

DAIMLER CVD 6

The Daimler CVD 6 (and its sisters CVA 6 and CVG 6) was to be among the longest lasting chassis types.

The original designation CV indicates Commercial Victory (chassis) with the engine type completing the coding - D6 = Daimler 6 - cylinder, A6 = AEC 6 - cylinder and G5 or G6 = Gardner 5 or 6 cylinder diesels and was introduced in 1946 as a relatively lightweight and updated variant on the war-time CW series.

That it remained in production until 1968 may be as much laid at the feet of conservative bus engineers as to any wish on Daimlers part.

Any city bus must be immensely strong, and although todays ramps and other traffic calming measures will eventually lead to chassis modifications these problems are only trifles compared with the cobbles, tramlines, bomb damage and raised man-hole covers commonplace when the CV chassis were first delivered to Birmingham Corporation Transport.

The frame is a relatively simple structure, the main components being numbered as in the drawing.

1. Frame side Member Assembly (offside)
2. Frame side Member Assembly (nearside)
3. Front Cross Tube Assembly
4. Front Spring Front Bracket (nearside)
5. Front Spring Front Bracket (offside)
6. Front Body Bracket (nearside)
7. Front Body Bracket (offside)
8. Intermediate Cross Tube Assembly
9. Gearbox Front Cross Tube Assembly
10. Gearbox Rear Cross Tube Assembly
11. Propeller Shaft Bridle Cross Member
12. Rear Spring Front Cross Member Assembly
13. Rear Spring Front Bracket
14. Rear Spring Rear Cross Member Assembly
15. Frame Stay Rear End
16. Rear Body Bracket Assembly (offside)
17. Rear Body Bracket Assembly (nearside)

However these assemblies totalled 101 components, with around half these being bolts and studs. A curiosity (and added in ink) is the requirement for a 'Destination Board Assembly' which came with the towing hook assembly, and was used to carry a slip-board across the radiator.

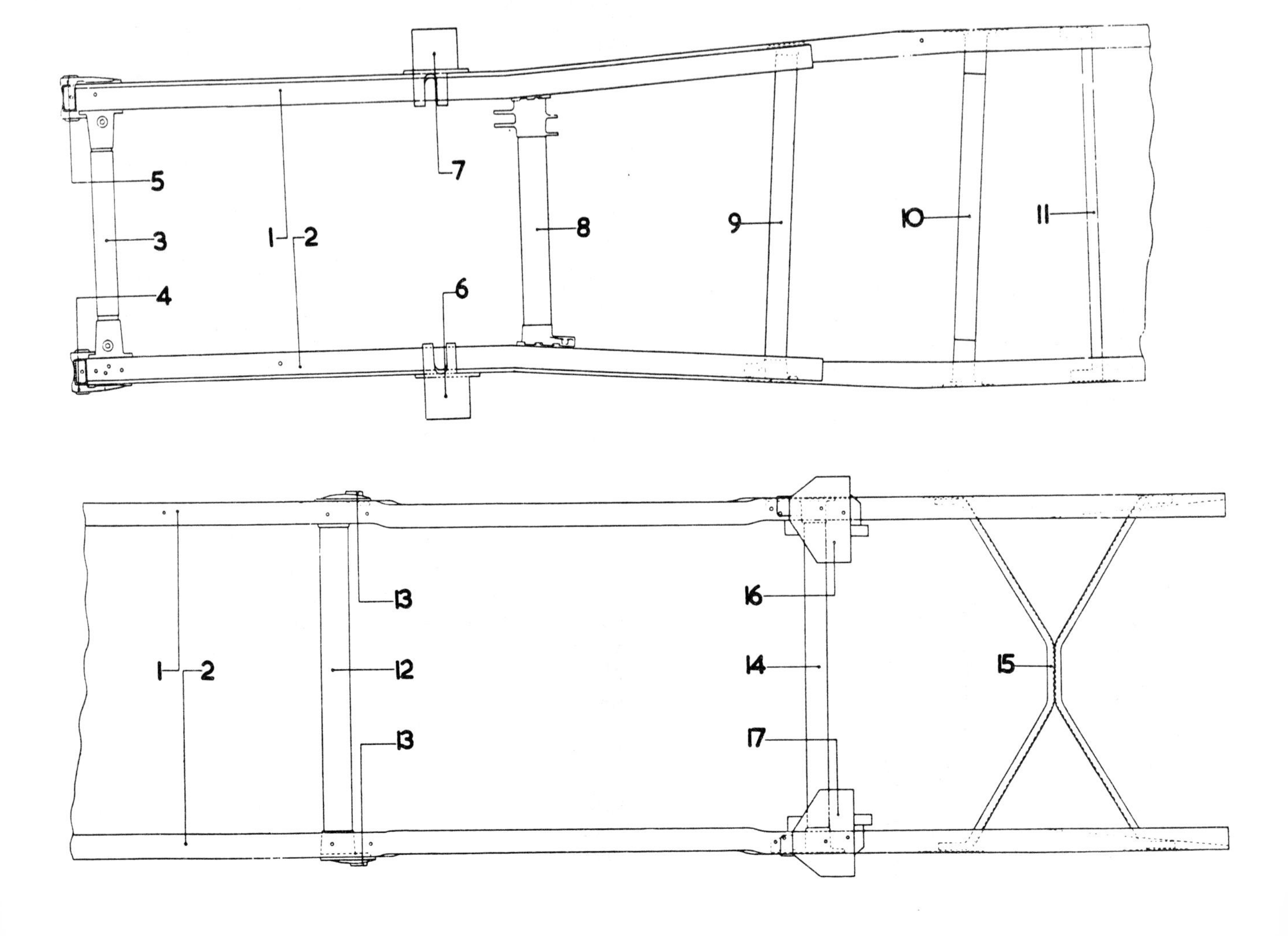

The radiator was another massive (and heavy) component and the exploded drawing shows some of its 96 parts. Added in ink is another BCT fitting "Radiator Muff - Weathershields - BCT Patt [ern]"

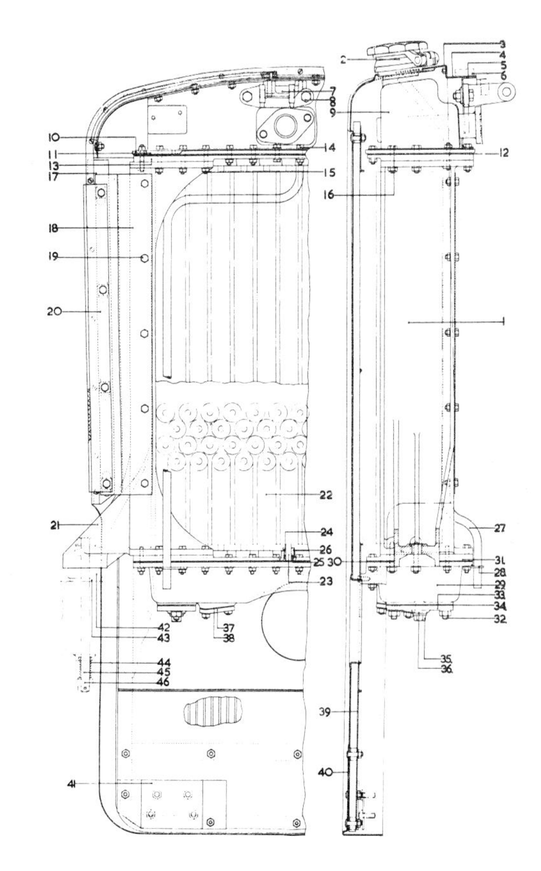

The CD 6 engine was the culmination of some years of research which, despite bombing, was carried on both in Coventry and various 'shadow' factories. Its apparent complexity belies the fact that it was one of the most reliable and useful engines ever produced, albeit rather heavier on fuel than the Gardner equivalent. In all there are nearly 700 components in this 8.6 litre 1948 variant and it never ceases to surprise me that given the living conditions, rationing and lack of general amenities in the decade after Britain 'won' the war the workmanship on these engines was such that they could run for 100,000 plus miles with only basic attention.

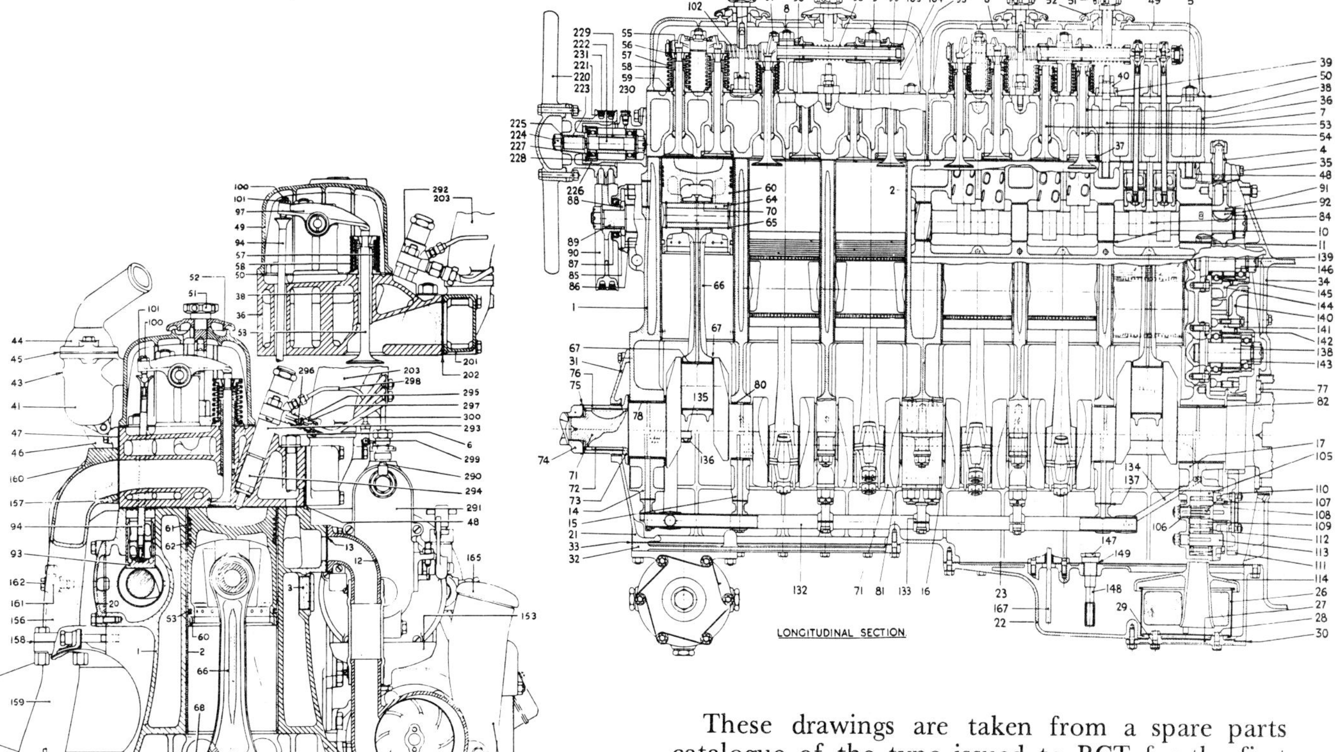

These drawings are taken from a spare parts catalogue of the type issued to BCT for the first 425 chassis supplied to them, and therefore the photographs reflect this. None of the machines shown, which were all bodied in the famous Birmingham 'Standard' style as 54 seaters by Metro-Cammell-Weymann at Saltley, Birmingham had a life of less than fifteen years with the Corporation, many from these batches going on to see further service either with other operators or as lorries. The quality of the whole machine is reflected by their weighing (with Met-Cam body) over 8 tons, rather more than their pre-war predecessors.

1
MAYPOLE
VIA BALSALL HEATH
48
VERNONS
HOV 969

2
STECHFORD
VIA DERITEND
54
HOV 782

3
29A
BANK
BANK
GENTLEMEN
HOV 803

4

PHOTOGRAPHS 1 - 4

Some of the regular haunts for Birmingham's CVD 6s.

PHOTOGRAPH 5

Although CVP 207 is a pre-war COG 5 nonetheless this is one of the few preserved vehicles to carry a destination slip-board, as here at the Midland Bus Museum, Wythall in 1992. HOV 685 is a Brush bodied Leyland PD2/1, JOJ 976 a Guy Arab 6 LW.

5

SCALED-DOWN OPERATIONS - THE STORY OF BEDFORD'S J2

by Fleet Scribbler

The dawning of the 1950s marked the start of an era of change for Bedford, undoubtedly one of Britain's most significant manufacturers of coaches of the time. The short-lived but rapidly outdating Bedford OB series of normal control, mid-capacity buses and coaches was earmarked for supercedence by the introduction of the SB range in 1950: a forward-control chassis capable of carrying 33-seat bodywork equipped with a superior power unit in the form of a 4.92 Bedford petrol unit. Variations on the SB chassis were still in production over three decades later, and several thousand examples were completed between the first 7'6" wide Duple Vega bodied examples and the last 8' wide Plaxton bodies examples produced in 1985.

But what of Bedford's smaller passenger carrying range of this time? The CA range of vans was soon converted to bus and coach work, with the resulting OLAZ, CAS and CAL series of public service vehicles being popular products between 1952 and 1968. 1957 marked the introduction of a chassis capable of 30-seat bodywork mounting: based on the C4Z and C5Z Bedford goods chassis, the C4Z1, C4Z2 and C5Z1 were only produced until 1961.

Completing the Bedford range from 1958 was another truck-derived chassis, based upon the new J-series. Available in a number of formats (differing chassis lengths, engine types and driver position), this allowed operators a tailor-made vehicle with standard delivery. The normal control model was known as the Bedford J3L, whilst the forward-control version on the same wheelbase of 13' 11" became the J4LZ. A shorter wheelbase measuring 9' 11" was launched as the J2SZ series, this forward-control chassis being the first non-van derived Bedford model to cater for the smaller vehicle market in post-war production.

The Bedford J2 models were equipped as standard with either a 3.52 litre, six-cylinder petrol engine (J2SZ2 specification) or a 3.14 litre 4-cylinder heavy oil version, although this latter unit was updated in 1960 to 3.29 litres, and again in 1967 to 3.61 litres (J2SZ10 specification). A four-speed synchromesh manual gearbox, effective vacuum hydraulic and a simple 12 volt electrical system completed the chassis package, which was suitable for carrying bodywork for up to 20 passengers. Throughout the production life of nearly two decades, nearly all of the chassis were then presented for bodywork fitting by one of three coachbuilders.

Plaxtons of Scarborough were responsible for the bodywork application to some two-thirds of all Bedford J2s produced, using their popular Plaxton Embassy III format. Designed as a replacement for their Consort V bodywork for smaller passenger vehicles, the bodywork styling on those examples completed prior to 1965 was visibly different to later coaches. Early types were typically glazed with two piece front and rear screens with curved extremes to a greater depth nearer the waist than the roof: later counterparts employed inter-changeable one-piece screens whose curvature did not intrude upon the sides of the body. The majority of the Embassies produced incorporated a tinted panoramic roof light to the fore, and an opening skylight positioned centrally: the generous glazing gave the impression of a light and spacious vehicle.

Usually equipped with twenty coach seats, a single courier seat was incorporated in front of the sliding nearside entrance door: a smaller driver's door (also the emergency exit) was immediately opposite. The exterior appearance of the Plaxton J2 was made all the more noticeable by the abundant use of chrome - as was usual for Plaxton designs of this era - a large oval shaped radiator grille with inset headlights above a chrome bumper at the front, two rear light clusters with a pointed, protruding chrome surround, and no less than three sets of rubber inlaid chrome bumping strips along each side - all complemented by four chrome plated or stainless steel wheel covers.

The bodywork format applied by Duple Midland possessed a more basic external appearance when compared with its Plaxton counterpart. The metal-framed "Compact" design utilised similar door positions to the Embassy, although the main entrance comprised a conventional outward-opening manual door. It was common for three sets of roof lights to be installed along the length of the body, extra light being necessary to compensate for the relatively small side windows. The seating capacity of the Compact was typically 15, with some potential capacity having been lost against the Plaxton Embassy by the provision of a rear shelf behind the rearmost seats. To the front of the coach, the radiator grille carried the distinctive Duple shield, whilst the headlights and sidelights were positioned either side. Unlike the Plaxton Embassy, whose spare wheel was stowed inside the rear luggage locker, the Compact hung its spare under the boot, consequently reducing the luggage capacity.

The 1960s connections between Duple Midland and Willowbrook were noticeably visible when studying the latter's bodywork styling for the J2, Duple Midland having acquired Willowbrook in 1960. To the same dimensions as Duple's Compact, the Willowbrook was developed as a service bus for Government departments and the Ministry of Defence: low back plastic seating emphasising this usage. An unusual entrance door arrangement allowed the driver to operate the two-piece centrally hinged doors by a crude linkage arrangement that passed around the front of the vehicle under the dashboard. A standard design prevailed throughout the remainder of the vehicle: there was no provision for a boot, no roof lights and a simple, hard-wearing interior decor.

Aside from the three main bodywork applications detailed thus far, several other well known companies experimented with unusual formats on this short chassis. Caetano enjoyed a brief flirtation with the J2 in the mid 1970s, offering a 20-seat body with full height windows and a flat roof, eliminating the need for roof cants. However, improved seating and an electric door did distinguish this bodywork from the earlier, more primitive Plaxton Embassy and Duple Compact. The end product did not sell too well, largely due to its box-like appearance at a time when full size, modern coaches were becoming available at reasonable prices, and only a very few survived into the 1990s. Northern Ireland coach-builder, Wrights of Ballymena also produced an angular body that never entered mainstream production. A flat, two-piece windscreen over a large chrome grille produced a rather plain frontal image, although the side roof cants and the outward opening door as applied to Duple's Compact were still in evidence.

The J2 was manufactured between 1958 and 1976. This functional little vehicle found immediate favour with the smaller independent operator, who required a coach for work where loadings did not warrant a full size vehicle but where there was still a need for a degree of comfort. Whilst soon a part of several well known independent fleets such as Frames Rickards, Marsh Motors, Armchair of London and Cleverly of Cwmbran, the J2 was never incorporated into the fleets of regional municipalities nor the subsidiary fleets of the National Bus Company. A number of overseas orders saw the J2 leaving these shores in the 1960s, the most significant of which was for Duple-bodied buses for Cypriot operator Lefkaritis.

Amongst the Government Departments that also specified the Bedford J2 as suitable for specific requirements was the Ministry of Defence, who found the functional and economic performance of the type to be ideal for various duties within the Royal Navy. The end of 1965 witnessed the first Plaxton bodied buses entering service, followed by a batch of Duples four years later. The largest order received were a consignment of Willowbrook service buses between 1969 and 1972, for almost exclusive use within naval bases. Other Government requirements favouring this smaller vehicle included the Atomic Energy and Research Establishment (A.E.R.E.) at Harwell, the Home Office, the Property Services Agency (P.S.A.), and the Prisons Department. The B.O.A.C. also employed Duple Midland coaches at Heathrow Airport in the latter half of the 1960s, although these differed from standard in having a large internal luggage pen towards the rear.

The number of operational Bedford J2s still earning their living in the 1990s is unfortunately very small, and some of the more significant survivors are detailed below. Norfolk-based Reynolds of Caister-on-Sea still provides gainful employment for Plaxton bodied NEB 606H and UVE 593K, whilst the challenging gradients of South Wales are the playground of MUR 202H with Watts of South Glamorgan and PEG 277G with Perry of Blackwood. Parkes of Lye have retained FEG 887K for occasional use, as have Hyke of Lincoln with their Plaxton bodied RJE 469J; nearby Yorkshire sees Ross of Featherstone with Plaxton bodied GGB 640L, whilst Wilkinson Garage of Kettlewell have only recently withdrawn their two examples which were retained for school contract work. An unusual Duple survivor is 1964 example BFP 209B with Smiths of Bracknell, Berkshire. Of the four Plaxton examples which were delivered new with a wheelchair lift and a reduced seating capacity so as to be able to accommodate wheelchairs, LAK 118G is used by Colclough of Southampton (who, incidentally, is also restoring the unique former Hillcrest Radio Coaches example XUM 123J), VZC 783 is still in use with the Irish Wheelchair Association of Clarinbridge, and MVE 400H is utilised by Storey's of Ely in East Anglia for the nearby Tower Hospital.

Still active, having escaped early retirement by becoming youth group transport are three further vehicles: PYU 11F (formerly with White, London) is in use in Dorset by 3rd Parkstone Scouts, former M.O.D. vehicle FWK 783Y is similarly with 7th Rugby Scouts, whilst Willowbrook bodied BTJ 262X has switched military loyalties: originally a Royal Navy vehicle, it now serves the Air Training Corps in Wigan!

The increasing ranks of preserved Bedford J2s will allow this unusual vehicle to last into the 21st Century. Again, Plaxton domination prevails: viz 884 GFU (ex Barry's Cabs, Norton), 643 HAA (ex Cookes, Guildford), 7209 PW (ex Jones, Downham Market), AMM 56A (re-registered, ex Collins, Hemingborough), BWD 858B (ex Cleverly, Cwmbran), MUR 200H (ex Frames Rickards), LDT 627K (ex Limehouse, Stockport): whilst 289 HWN, new to Bawdens Coaches, claims to be owned by the Half Moon Inn Bus Preservation Society, Northchapel (near Guildford), although it has never attended a rally and is used solely for pub crawls! XUM 123J, new to Shilton of Leeds and later modified by Hillcrest Radio Coaches of Alvechurch to give a unique front and rear styling, was purchased out of preservation by Colclough of Southampton in early 1994, and will be returned to P.S.V. use in due course.

The Duple Midland stock of preservation candidates is now alarmingly low. North-east based PYY 28D is believed to be the only example preserved, following the unfortunate malicious vandalism and subsequent scrapping of 379 BXM. The latter coach was the oldest survivor of the type, being new to Roy Bowles Transport of Heathrow in 1961. There are currently no examples of the Caetano or Willowbrook vehicles held as preserved: of the latter, UVP 94S (originally Royal Navy 12 RN 77) was purchased in 1993 but subsequently scrapped due to a very weak chassis structure after many years of corrosion.

With the modern trends set by the New Age Traveller fuelling the demand for suitable vehicles for conversion to mobile caravans, it is not too surprising to note that the trusty J2s have undergone some rather unorthodox conversions in the last decade, and it is unfortunate for many that this is a one-way journey and many are lost or become untraceable as a result. A selection of those still known to exist at the present time are as follows: RTE 239L (Plaxton, noted Pilton, Somerset), ABD 699A (Plaxton, noted Llanbister, Mid Glamorgan), JPN 110D, (Duple, noted Pilton, Somerset), LPN 735E (Duple, noted Ibstock, Leics.), JCP 215F (Plaxton, noted Eye, Suffolk), CHA 875Y (Willowbrook, and JCH 380N and Q748 LPP (Plaxtons, noted Leicester). Two Plaxton examples particularly worthy of mention are 3037 WY, which has had the upper half of a Commer panel van grafted onto its roof, whilst XEL 758B similarly has an early split-screen Volkswagen Transporter in the same position!

Aside from serviceable J2s, their preserved counterparts and the pot-pourri of caravans, a few examples have survived to fulfil altogether more unusual occupations. Plaxton bodied AYN 41B is currently owned by a garage in Loughborough for publicity purposes, whilst former Guide Friday Plaxton coach KHA 292E is likewise employed in Ellistown. Duple-bodied HBC 987D has been converted to become a car transporter - no easy task when one considers how small the J2 is, whereas NHL 149F is a Plaxton coach that provides the transport for a pop group in Oldham!

With less than 50 examples of the Bedford J2 surviving today, their continued existence is constantly threatened by vehicles being scrapped or converted to caravans. It is, however, reassuring to note that several coaches appear to have a secure future in the hands of caring preservationists: a living reminder of one of Britain's original minibuses . . . . and we all know how popular minibuses are to today's bus industry!

643 HAA - J2SZ10 Plaxton C18F. Leighfield, Grittenham (Preserved)(New to Cookes, Guildford) Woburn Showbus 1992.

[J.A. Godwin]

Godwin, Merstham (Preserved). XUM 123J J2SZ10 Plaxton C20F (varied from C16 to C20 according to duties) - ex Hillcrest Radio Coaches. Sevenoaks Bus Station: Kentish Rally. 1.8.93. Alongside is MUR 200H, J2SZ10 now preserved but new to Frames Rickards.

[J.A. Godwin]

Worthing, February 1992. 379 BXM J2S22 Duple C15F. New to Roy Bowles, Heathrow.

[J.A. Godwin]

J2SZ2 petrol engine, 14 seats delivered new 9 June 1970.

[Plaxtons Ltd.]

J2SZ10/Caetano C20F. Wacton, Bromyard 31/12/93. Ex Plymouth Operator.

[J.A. Godwin]

386 DD - J2SZ10 Plaxton C17F. Ex Marsh's Coaches. Now Wacton, Bromyard. September 1992.

[J.A. Godwin]

Southampton Docks, June 1993. Colclough, Southampton. J2SZ2 1964. Plaxton 11 seats plus fixed wheelchair lift.

[J.A. Godwin]

J2SZ10/Duple B18F. September 1964. Bus variant.

[Unknown]

XRP 368S (re-registered ex Ministry of Defence) J2SZ2 Willowbrook B19F. Ludlows of Halesowen, March 1990.

[D.D. Gladwin]

J2SZ10 Caetano C20F - MTM 76P. Ashtree Coaches 1989.

[D.D. Gladwin]

COUNTRY BODIES

In bus and coach bodybuilding terms, certain major firms automatically spring to mind - Duple, Plaxton, Burlingham, Park Royal, Roe, Eastern Coach Works, Alexander, Metro-Cammell-Weymann and so on. One can then add those companies who built both chassis and bodies - Leyland, Crossley, Dennis and Bristol (as BBW). In all, around 25 concerns. Postwar (and in some cases for very short periods indeed) came another 30 odd whose names have, at least, been recorded or whose products lasted long enough to be photographed.

Before 1939 the picture was quite different as although the road wagon-cum-coach-builders of the 1920s had faded away there were a surprising number of car or railway wagon bodyshops who would by one means or another obtain orders, often for one-offs. Some perhaps were got by competitive pricing although it was rare that they could realistically compete value-for-value - with even medium sized companies, others as the directors of both the bus operator and the body builders were members of the same Masons Lodge or, and this happened regularly, they might quote a combination of "you can keep an eye on it being built as we are local", sharp pricing and quick delivery. Alternatively they might offer very, very good H.P. terms to get the work. Advertisements of a few years ago by coach-builders for 'Interest free credit' gave one a ghastly feeling of deja-vu.

Cross and Ellis of Coventry was an independent coachbuilding firm who commenced operations in 1919 mainly building bespoke bodies on upmarket chassis, making a speciality of bodying Alvis. In 1927 they had 220 employees and produced around 30 finished cars per week but by 1931 the signs of depression within the motor industry were all too apparent, with Cross and Ellis's main chassis suppliers, Alvis and Lea Francis going into liquidation leaving them in the mire for cash. As a result they took on any work that could be got, alas not entirely successfully. The following is quoted from Vintage Style, by Gillian Bardsley (Brewin Books 1993) and illustrates just how a small bodybuilder coped when they moved outside their usual field.

BUILDING A COACH

Doug Pettifer [body-maker 1932-1937] also remembered the process of building a coach, which involved a great deal of extra effort:

"A previous coach they couldn't get out the door. They got it a bit too high to go through the door. So what they had to do was to get everybody available to come and sit in the thing to weight it down and somebody standing on a high ladder and watching it as it was driven gently out . . . The only one that I worked on, complete to build, was I think the last one that Cross & Ellis built, about 1932. It was on a Reo chassis for a coach firm in Rugby. It was about a 28-seater, a relatively small coach. But the first thing we made on that was the roof. Dad got the contract for this you see, and that was actually running alongside Alvis work as well. Occupied a lot of space. And the first thing my dad says, "We'll make the roof". "What first?" He says, "Yes, then we can keep dry while we're doing the rest can't we?" . . . We made this roof, it was for all the world like a big boat, the shape of the coach. It was made with a wood frame round the outside, the rim, the camp rail as it was called and the cross form was going across it, giving you the shape that way which you could see in any coach at the time or any tramcar or bus if you looked up. Then the top of it was covered in and when that was done . . . all this was covered over with match-boarding. The ends were covered over with metal panels where it had got a double curvature, the panel beaters made us some metal panels for that. And we made the roof complete and you could literally have floated it like a boat if you'd wanted to. I don't say it would be very negotiable but it would have floated alright. And huge. I said, "Why did you make the roof first?" and he says, "how do you think we're going to get these boards on if we have it up in the air. It's much easier to do it down here like this." Of course it was. So when we'd got the frame of the coach made - lots of pillars all the way down it, every two foot six or so between the glasses, like a coach is now only it's metal - when we got that frame on, then we had as many people as we could get with ladders and steps and boxes and lord knows what and we got this roof and we sort of fed it on from the back. And we worked it on until we got it in position, then of course we fixed it on to the top. But of course, there was no work to do on that, it was done. What did have to be done, which wasn't our pigeon then, when it was on, the trimmers came and they covered it over with white canvas. They tacked it neatly round all the edges tight, drum-tight. Then we glued it all over, right over the lot, canvas as well, hot glue, you know what hot gelatine glue's like, we used no end of it. Covered it all over with this and - I can see it now - standing on ladders we were swabbing this on with rags, with our hands, putting them into the hot glue and swashing it on. Dad was saying "rub it well in" and we had to rub it through, right through to the canvas to the wood below it. And then when it was dry next day we went over it lightly with sandpaper and got all the little bits and pieces off and said "Oh, it's beautifully tight, drum tight". Then the painters painted it and they put on half a dozen coats at least of white lead paint, so that it was absolutely impervious to anything that the heavens could send down. And that was the roof. And it was ultimately done with black at the top, but it was the lead paint underneath that did the work. The black on top, that did nothing. I remember again, we dropped a clanger on that, when the coach had to go to be checked by the Ministry of Transport, or whoever it was. It had to go to Birmingham to be checked for measurements.

The Works, 1923 - Sawmill

There were certain measurements which had to be obeyed, right size seats, right distance between them and so on, right headroom. Well we'd made this as I remember quite well, five foot ten height, which was the height it had to be inside, walking room. A six foot man had to stoop a bit, or take his shoes off. So the last thing, one of the last things I did, dad brought me some strips of wood. "Here", he says, "put these down the gangway of the coach". It had been covered with lino. "Screw them all on two inches apart - get a couple of blocks of wood that width so then you won't have to measure all the while. Put the middle one down first and then work outwards". So I found the middle and put one strip down the middle then put the others all the way down, screwed down every foot or so into the wooden floor and in due course this went away to be inspected. When it came back, among other minor things, "head-room, half inch short. Registers five foot nine and a half, must be five foot ten." So my dad says, "you'd better get them treads stripped off," so that's what I had to do."

Cross and Ellis closed in 1938. All the cutting and assembly of components within a concern of that size was necessarily hand work as a 'run' of car bodies might be no more than a handful, whereas a coach body-builder might cut the frames for 20 or more bodies and when the men were quiet have them complete stackable subassemblies.

Another great advantage of a large body-builder was, having a full time drawing office, they could show design flexibility but even when building a 'standard' shell the men would work to detail drawings thus almost eliminating time and money wasting problems typified by those found by Cross and Ellis.

Strachans (who went through various manifestations) were one firm who tried to lead from the front, the following appearing in **Motor Transport** 12 January 1931, which is of particular interest due to the early use of duralumin. The vehicles were mounted on Maudslay ML3B chassis and still extant on the outbreak of war, albeit probably disused.

"Two interesting 32-seater bodies have been built recently by Strachans (Acton)Ltd., for Robson Brothers, of High Spen, Co. Durham. The outstanding feature of these bodies is their light weight, the total body weight being 25 cwt [1270 kg], including such refinements as well-upholstered seats, a sliding door at the front, a fully enclosed cab, and an automatic step below the rear emergency door. This low weight has been made possible by the wide use of duralumin for such metal parts as cross-bearers, flitch plates, corner brackets, drop window frames, floor slats, commode handles, and the like". Perhaps rather surprisingly, the Saunders-Roe 'Rivaloy' or 'Saro' body which embodied all the advances of 22 years of vehicle construction and aircraft building knowledge weighed 36¼ cwt [1842 kg] (albeit for a 44 seater) in 1953.

The following selection of photographs is intended to give the flavour of various periods; most but not all the bodies came from small, or at least, 'homely' body-builders and are a far cry from today's sophisticated machines whose lines are air tunnel and computor generated and which are, in the main, built in clinically clean metal working factories.

40 h.p. Fiat with North Eastern Railway 34 seat body c. 1908. Behind is a Saurer 30 h.p.

Fiat again, showing her real char-a-banc body c.1909.

"The Alma" (FM 387) was a 1911 Dennis with bodywork by Henry Eaton of Manchester. No. 2 in Crosville's fleet it was sold in 1919 but survived another couple of years.

This strange looking bus EA 999, No. 5 in the fleet of West Bromwich Corporation had Roberts of West Bromwich bodywork on a Tillings Stevens TS3 chassis. Seating 29 it survived (albeit with much rebuilding) from 1920 to 1930.

The Pride of Burnley. No. 1 in the motor bus fleet was a Leyland A13 with 1924 Leyland Bodywork fitted with rather unusual tram-like longitudinal seating. Later rebuilt No. 1 was scrapped in 1936.

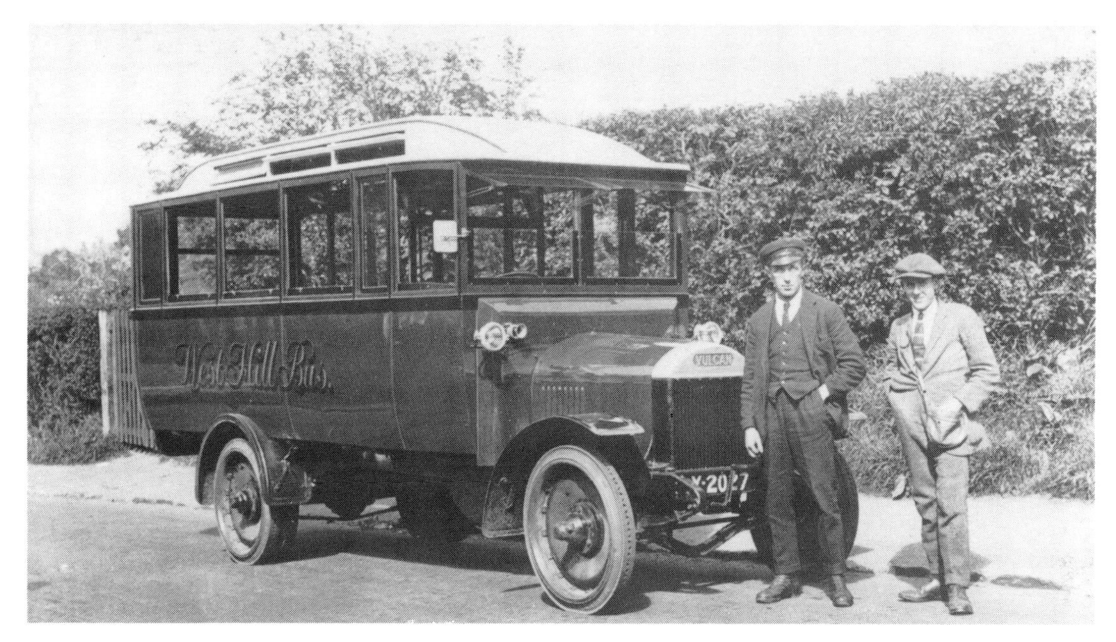

A Vulcan of around the same period belonging to West Hill Bus. The similarity of the driver's uniform to that of railwaymen and the clerestory roof give a delightful period feel.

[D.W.K. Jones]

A 1925 Albion PW24 belonging to Hicks Bros. Although pneumatic tyres have improved comfort, a 'rag-top' body like this was quickly outdated and it was re-bodied as a lorry in 1930.

A marvelous example of 'country bus' thinking albeit with bodywork by Strachans of Acton on a Dennis chassis. The combination of disappearing roof and luggage rack is neat, but since speed was limited to 12 m.p.h. (20 k.p.h.) it must be pre-1928.

Blue Bus Reo with Taylor bodywork in service 1928-1933.

The 'Blue Comfy Cars' Reo in Swanage High Street in 1932 was true of the first word but probably not the second; the long wheelbase with a short body was typical of American imports.
[R.W. Kidner]

The 'Elite' worked from Cassio Road to Bushey Lane, Watford, joining London Country in August 1933. This Chevrolet with its odd central headlight and lightweight Smith's bodywork typified independants of the 1930s.

'Aberdare Red' Willys No. CC9402 at Pwllheli in 1931 is not as old as it looks, as the registration indicates.
[R.W. Kidner]

Strachans of Acton bodywork again, on a Berliet chassis. Most importantly this is a 'Safety Coach' replacing plate glass windows with toughened 'unshatterable' ones.

UR 6298, No. 411 in the Crosville fleet which operated joint services with the London Midland & Scottish Railway had a 23 seat Watsons of Lowestoft body on an Albion PM28 chassis and entered service April 1930.

A year earlier IJ 9513 first ran on the bus routes of the Belfast & County Down Railway. The design appears quite crude but the bodywork was built by Vulcan of Southport on a Vulcan VWBL chassis but was withdrawn in 1935.

[R.C. Ludgate]

After the Second World War it was almost as if all the dormant country bus bodybuilders, whose numbers were decimated in the 1930s, suddenly came back to life, although in reality most were diversifying after losing war contracts. Associated Coach Builders of Southwick, near Sunderland seems to have had pre-war ancestry and their designs reflected this; here we have a 1951 Dennis Lancet J3 (later registered LPT 236) bodied for Robbins of Easington Lane, who one feels must have shuddered at that front end, while the rear merely looks old-fashioned.

In 1936 Pioneer Service of Cudworth took delivery of their latest 'little gem' on an Albion Victor chassis.

This unfortunate body is on a Bedford chassis, non-PSV for Lewisham, London, Borough Council and was photographed in 1982. The bodywork - which could have appeared in 1925 - was by Strachans albeit by now they had moved to Hamble, near Southampton.

[D. Stevenson]

— The Bus Crews —

They Really Are People!

DRIVER'S DAY BY ADSUM

The working day of a driver varies according to the mores of his Superintendant, the general discipline within the garage and on the staff situation. This may all sound self-evident, but each and every reader, professional or otherwise, will know of different methods of working. To quote an obvious example, London Transport had the largest standardized fleet of diesel engined buses in the World, but although the whole maintenance, fuelling and cleaning concept may have been laid down from above, local conditions required local adaptions. Or, on the other hand, two Municipals may buy identical vehicles, identical even to the bodywork and each have a totally different approach to servicing or cleaning.

Drivers represent to office staff a difficult, if not intractable, problem insofar as they keep wanting better conditions. No one, but no one really likes split shifts and at one time there were some real horrors. Given an 8½ hour day was it alright, or fair, to expect a man to work 06.30 - 09.00, then 11.30 - 14.00 and to finish his day from 16.00 - 19.30? This was a real dog's life, truly a bite and a run. The driving conditions were horrendous with busy rush hour traffic met during all three segments and with little chance of a cup of tea during the turnarounds. Even the girls, who quite often swopped for a single split shift (am or pm) to take or collect their children or for shopping purposes, ran away from these. When the new Superintendant arrived, installed because of low morale and high wastage, all of a sudden the triple shifts, hitherto an absolutely vital two weeks in eight, were found to be unnecessary.

Because time off (shown as sickness) declined wages actually rose, and with them morale.

So, we shall assume that we have a driver of some standing in the garage, who has passed through the 'spare' or 'stand-by' link or roster and has an established turn. As this is not a garage normally affected by seasonal activities he will know his work for, probably, a 26 week cycle. Within this period will be a handful of split turns, and one or two weeks spare or relief work. Some drivers like this as, at its simplest, it means that they book on at a reasonable time and take out any turn available. Once they would not have been paid until a man 'knocked', now normal conditions and rates apply. Our "old hand" will, of course, be known to the roster clerk as one who will enjoy market-day work on 'The Track', an ex-tram route, where another will be far happier on a Special or country bus Route. Most 'Specials' are 'posted' on the board a day or two ahead but it may be that another garage cannot cover all their work and our man can be asked to cover this. It may be only the alternate working on the half-hour to our garages hourly service or it could be that none of their 'spare' men were passed out on all types of vehicles. Some, for example, will have learned to drive on an old crash-box Crossley or Guy, while later trainees only worked pre-select Daimlers and auto-box Leopards. Or their route-knowledge may have only covered the basic services.

Either way, working from another garage was nearly always voluntary and, regrettably, on occasions 'foreigners' who have turned up have been sent away again by Union Officials anxious to protect their Members overtime.

But we will assume our driver has had his job 'posted' as running sheet, board or chit number; 52 reporting at 11.50 am as in the example below. When he books on the time-keeper (often but not always an invalided out driver or conductor) will give him the vehicle number.

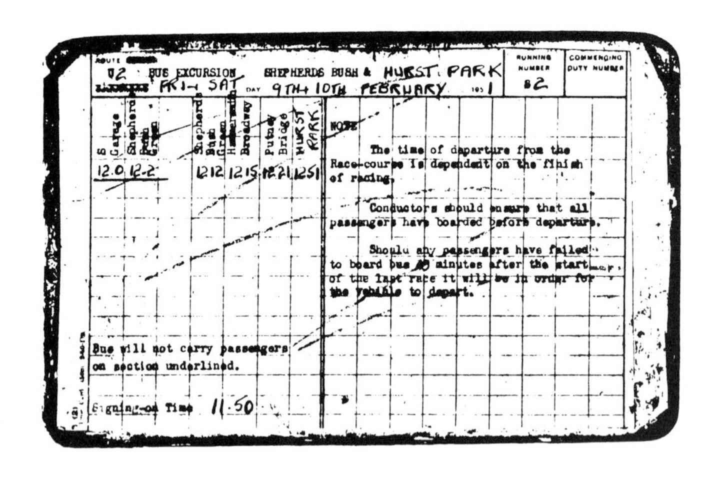

ROUTE 02 BUS EXCURSION SHEPHERDS BUSH & HURST PARK — RUNNING NUMBER 52 — COMMENCING DUTY NUMBER

FRI + SAT DAY 9TH + 10TH FEBRUARY 1951

Garage	Shepherds Bush Green	Shepherds Bush Green	Hammersmith Broadway	Putney Bridge	HURST PARK
12.0	12.2	12.12	12.15	12.21	12.51

NOTE

The time of departure from the Race-course is dependent on the finish of racing.

Conductors should ensure that all passengers have boarded before departure.

Should any passengers have failed to board bus 30 minutes after the start of the last race it will be in order for the vehicle to depart.

Bus will not carry passengers on section underlined.

Signing-on Time 11.50

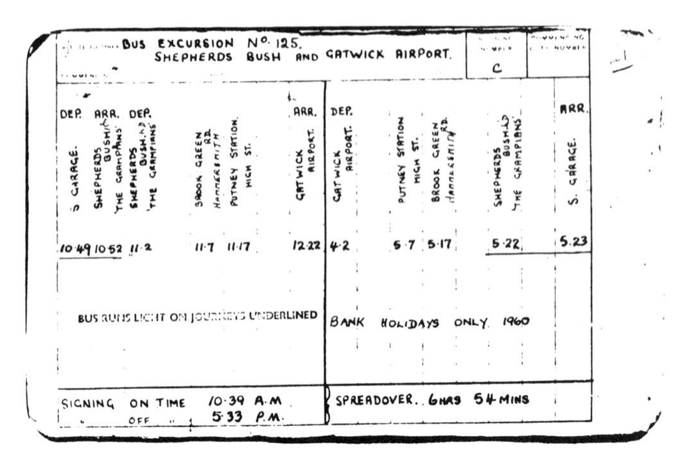

BUS EXCURSION No. 125.
SHEPHERDS BUSH AND GATWICK AIRPORT. — RUNNING NUMBER C — COMMENCING DUTY NUMBER

DEP. S. Garage	ARR. Shepherds Bush 'The Grampians'	DEP. Shepherds Bush 'The Grampians'	Brook Green Rd. Hammersmith	Putney Station High St.	ARR. Gatwick Airport
10.49	10.52	11.2	11.7	11.17	12.22

DEP. Gatwick Airport	Putney Station High St.	Brook Green Rd. Hammersmith	Shepherds Bush 'The Grampians'	ARR. S. Garage
4.2	5.7	5.17	5.22	5.23

BUS RUNS LIGHT ON JOURNEYS UNDERLINED

BANK HOLIDAYS ONLY 1960

SIGNING ON TIME 10.39 A.M.
" OFF " 5.33 P.M.

SPREADOVER. 6 HRS 54 MINS

This can be a garage plate number arranged in the order of departure (BX 44 is the 44th vehicle out that day) or the fleet number or the registration. It may be the Gaffer will just say 'take the Regal' if only one is visible. Water, oil and tyres checked, the driver will be joined by the conductor clutching either his machine or a rack of tickets plus a Bell Punch and his float and waybill. A good quality crew will always book in early, complete their respective duties and have a quiet relaxing cuppa before departure.

A later type of board is also shown and this is one of the double sided designs that can drive one to distraction. The main interest in this relates to the hours worked and the relative paucity of breaks. It is in fact a double duty the first crew booking on at 0704, being (on paper) relieved en route by the first turn of a split shift.

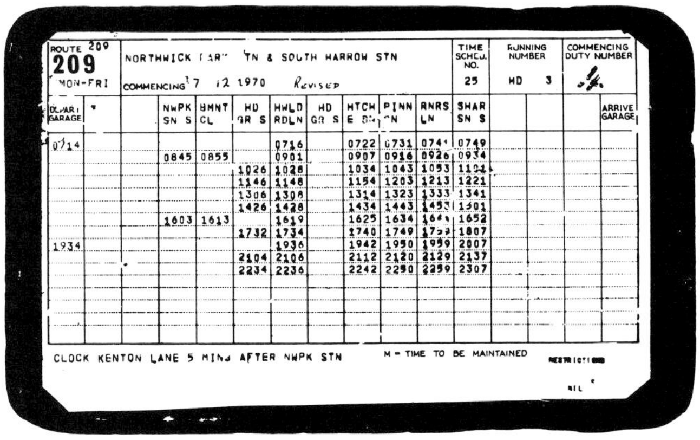

It was, and is, quite normal practice to be relieved at a traffic point. Of course, if you wish to be favourably regarded by the 'Main Man' at the garage (be he Superintendant or your local friendly Inspector) you could work right through the first turn . . . .

The next two running boards are of the modern plastic coated type and show a full days city-based work for a driver, with however a School Holidays variant.

ROUTE 209 — NORTHWICK PARK STN & SOUTH HARROW STN — MON-FRI — COMMENCING 7 12 1970 Revised — TIME SCHED. NO. 25 — RUNNING NUMBER HD 3 — COMMENCING DUTY NUMBER 4

DEPART GARAGE	*		NWPK SN S	BMNT CL	HD GR S	HWLD RDLN	HD GR S	HTCH E SN	PINN SN	RNRS LN	SHAR SN S	ARRIVE GARAGE
0714						0716		0722	0731	074[illegible]	0749	
			0845	0855		0901		0907	0916	0926	0934	
					1026	1028		1034	1043	1053	[illegible]	
					1146	1148		1154	1203	1213	1221	
					1306	1308		1314	1323	1333	1341	
					1426	1428		1434	1443	1453	1501	
			1603	1613		1619		1625	1634	164[illegible]	1652	
					1732	1734		1740	1749	17[illegible]	1807	
1934						1936		1942	1950	1959	2007	
					2104	2106		2112	2120	2129	2137	
					2234	2236		2242	2250	2259	2307	

CLOCK KENTON LANE 5 MINS AFTER NWPK STN — M = TIME TO BE MAINTAINED

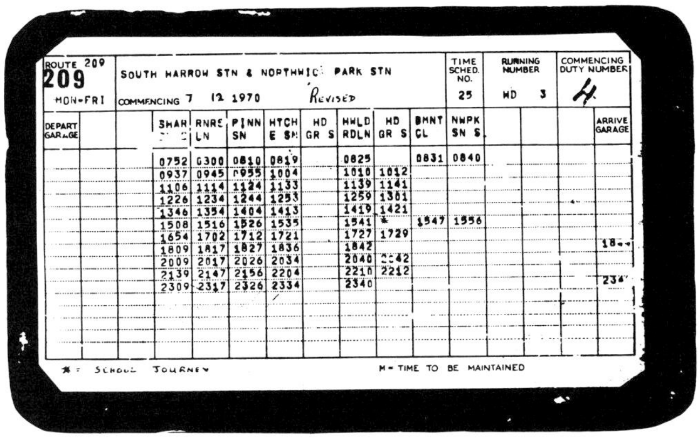

ROUTE 209 — SOUTH HARROW STN & NORTHWICK PARK STN — MON-FRI — COMMENCING 7 12 1970 Revised — TIME SCHED. NO. 25 — RUNNING NUMBER HD 3 — COMMENCING DUTY NUMBER 4

DEPART GARAGE			SHAR SN S	RNRS LN	PINN SN	HTCH E SN	HD GR S	HWLD RDLN	HD GR S	BMNT CL	NWPK SN S	ARRIVE GARAGE
			0752	0800	0810	0819		0825		0831	0840	
			0937	0945	0955	1004		1010	1012			
			1106	1114	1124	1133		1139	1141			
			1226	1234	1244	1253		1259	1301			
			1346	1354	1404	1413		1419	1421			
			1508	1516	1526	1535		1541	*	1547	1556	
			1654	1702	1712	1721		1727	1729			
			1809	1817	1827	1836		1842				18[illegible]
			2009	2017	2026	2034		2040	2042			
			2139	2147	2156	2204		2210	2212			
			2309	2317	2326	2334		2340				234[illegible]

* = SCHOOL JOURNEY — M = TIME TO BE MAINTAINED

DAYS OF OPERATION: Monday-Friday START DATE: 30/12/1991

DEPART BROMFORD LANE DEPOT 0750 AND RUN PRIVATE TO TILE CROSS

*** The correct blind for Lanchester Way is CHELMSLEY WOOD NORTH ***

RTE	TIMING POINT	ARR.	DEP.
810	TILE CROSS		0805
	Marston Green Stn		0808
	The Greenwood		0823
	Chelmsley Wood		0828
	Bluebell Drive		0833
	Coleshill School		0838
	C.HILL MIDDLE SCH	0843	
	Run Private To		
72	LANCHESTER WAY		0931
	Kingshurst		0939
	Chelmsley Wood		0949
	Marston Green Stn		0954
	Sheldon		1010
72	SOLIHULL STATION	1024	1038
	Sheldon		1052
	Marston Green Stn		1108
	Chelmsley Wood		1113
	Kingshurst		1123
72	LANCHESTER WAY	1130	1131
	Kingshurst		1139
	Chelmsley Wood		1149
	Marston Green Stn		1154
	Sheldon		1210
72	SOLIHULL STATION	1224	1238
	Sheldon		1252
	Marston Green Stn		1308
	Chelmsley Wood		1313
	Kingshurst		1323
72	LANCHESTER WAY	1330	1331
	Kingshurst		1339
	Chelmsley Wood		1349
	Marston Green Stn		1354
	Sheldon		1410
	SOLIHULL STATION	1424	
72E	SOLIHULL STATION		1438
	Sheldon		1452
	Marston Green Stn		1508
	CHELMSLEY WOOD	1513	
	Run Private To		
863	C.HILL MIDDLE SCH		1530
	COLESHILL High St	1536	
	Run Private To		
810	COLESHILL SCHOOL		1541
	Bluebell Drive		1546
	Chelmsley Wood		1551
	The Greenwood		1556
	Marston Green Stn		1611
	TILE CROSS	1614	
	Run Private To		
96	SHIRESTONE ROAD		1708
	The Mackadown		1711
	Stechford		1719
	Victoria Street		1728
96	CARRS LANE	1738	1740
	Victoria Street		1750
	Stechford		1759
	The Mackadown		1807
	Chelmsley Wood		1816
96	BLUEBELL DRIVE	1822	1832
	Chelmsley Wood		1837
	The Mackadown		1845
	Stechford		1853
	Victoria Street		1901
	CARRS LANE	1910	

- Cont'd -

Return to depot; Arrive at 1930 Running Board Number: 72-01

*** SCHOOL HOLIDAYS ONLY ***

DAYS OF OPERATION: Monday-Friday START DATE: 30/12/1991

DEPART BROMFORD LANE DEPOT 0916 AND RUN PRIVATE TO LANCHESTER WAY

*** The correct blind for Lanchester Way is CHELMSLEY WOOD NORTH ***

RTE	TIMING POINT	ARR.	DEP.
72	LANCHESTER WAY		0931
	Kingshurst		0939
	Chelmsley Wood		0949
	Marston Green Stn.		0954
	Sheldon		1010
72	SOLIHULL STATION	1024	1038
	Sheldon		1052
	Marston Green Stn.		1108
	Chelmsley Wood		1113
	Kingshurst		1123
72	LANCHESTER WAY	1130	1131
	Kingshurst		1139
	Chelmsley Wood		1149
	Marston Green Stn.		1154
	Sheldon		1210
72	SOLIHULL STATION	1224	1238
	Sheldon		1252
	Marston Green Stn.		1308
	Chelmsley Wood		1313
	Kingshurst		1323
72	LANCHESTER WAY	1330	1331
	Kingshurst		1339
	Chelmsley Wood		1349
	Marston Green Stn.		1354
	Sheldon		1410
	SOLIHULL STATION	1424	
72	SOLIHULL STATION		1438
	Sheldon		1452
	Marston Green Stn.		1508
	Chelmsley Wood		1513
	Kingshurst		1523
72	LANCHESTER WAY	1530	1531
	Kingshurst		1539
	Chelmsley Wood		1549
	Marston Green Stn.		1554
	Sheldon		1610
72	SOLIHULL STATION	1624	1638
	Sheldon		1652
	Marston Green Stn.		1708
	Chelmsley Wood		1713
	Kingshurst		1723
	LANCHESTER WAY	1730	

- Cont'd -

Return to depot; Arrive at 1745 Running Board Number: 72-01

The final sheet - one could hardly grace it with the name of board - was one produced for a proposed new country bus service and is mainly of interest as it was generated entirely by a computor, based on a timetable which was also calculated by a computor! In all probability it would have worked, but was not deemed to be financially viable.

Bedlington "Blue" Bus Company

VEHICLE RUNNING BOARD

Tuesday Only.

Service	Stage point	Arr.	Dep.	Notes
	Depot		0830	Empty
❷	Worcester, Crowngate	0845	0850	
	Alfrick, Swan		0917	
	Suckley, Stocks Cross		0929	
	Bishops Frome		0941	
	Bosbury, Bell		1000	
	Wellington Heath, Oak Tree		1015	
⓿	Ledbury, Market Hall	1025	1026	Empty
	Gloucester Road Island	1028	1030	
❷	Ledbury, Memorial	1032	1050	
	Wellington Heath, Oak Tree		1100	
	Bosbury, Bell		1115	
	Bishops Frome		1135	
	Suckley, Stocks Cross		1147	
	Alfrick, Swan		1159	
	Worcester, Crowngate	1230		
		1235	1325	RTA Break
❷	Worcester, Crowngate		1330	
	Alfrick, Swan		1357	
	Suckley, Stocks Cross		1409	
	Bishops Frome		1421	
	Bosbury, Bell		1440	
	Wellington Heath, Oak Tree		1455	
⓿	Ledbury, Market Hall	1505	1506	Empty
	Gloucester Road Island	1508	1510	
❷	Ledbury Memorial	1512	1520	
	Wellington Heath, Oak Tree		1530	
	Bosbury, Bell		1545	
	Bishops Frome		1605	
	Suckley, Stocks Cross		1617	
	Alfrick, Swan		1629	
⓿	Worcester, Crowngate	1700	1705	Empty
	Depot	1720		

Booking off in the days of conductors was relatively simple. Either the driver would be relieved at a traffic point, amble back to the garage, book off or - in a small garage - wake up the timekeeper long enough for him to tick off your return. If the vehicle was brought back it may or may not have been the responsibility of the driver to put it through the wash, fill the tank with diesel then stable it, as there may be ferry-men.

Items on the bus requiring repair were either entered in a book, the mechanic signing it off on completion, or on check sheets which the driver signed, or a chit was completed and handed to the timekeepers. Or you may just tell Fred!

With the advent of one-person-operation the driver will collect his ticket machine when booking on, but may not have to complete a waybill as these are produced electronically and he may indeed not touch any cash. One firm and no doubt many others leave the machines permanently on the vehicle, the driver merely inserting a personalised key to activate it.

ROUTE 43

BUS PASSES, LT CARDS AND TRAVELCARDS

VALID IN ZONE/AREA	ARE AVAILABLE BETWEEN
BARNET 4(5/6)	FRIERN BARNET 1 and WILTON ROAD 3
3	WILTON ROAD 3 and ARCHWAY Station 8
2	WATERLOW ROAD 8 and ISLINGTON 13
1	ISLINGTON 13 and LONDON BRIDGE 20 or LIVERPOOL STREET 29

THE FARES SHOWN APPLY ONLY WHEN THROUGH JOURNEYS ARE SHOWN

CHILD FARES

FROM 0300 TO 0929 MONDAYS TO FRIDAYS (except public holidays): **40p**

FROM 2200 to 0259 DAILY: ADULT FARE

AT ALL OTHER TIMES: **30p**

FOR CHILD AND TRAVEL PERMIT CONDITIONS SEE OVER

AFTER 0929 MONDAYS TO FRIDAYS UNTIL 0300 THE FOLLOWING DAY, AND ALL DAY SATURDAYS, SUNDAYS AND PUBLIC HOLIDAYS

80p & £1.00 fares reduced to.... **60p**

£1.50 fares reduced to.... **£1.10**

Stage	Fares	Stage point
1		FRIERN BARNET Town Hall 1
2	40	NORTH CIRCULAR ROAD 2
3	40 40	WILTON ROAD Minstrel Boy 3
4	40 40 40	MUSWELL HILL BROADWAY Queens Avenue 4
5	60 40 40 | 40	CRANLEY GARDENS 5
6	80 60 40 | 40 40	HIGHGATE Station 6
7	80 80 60 | 40 40 40	WINCHESTER HALL TAVERN 7
8	80 80 60 | 60 40 40 | 40	WATERLOW ROAD or ARCHWAY Station 8 †
9	100 80 80 | 80 60 40 | 40 40	HOLLOWAY ROAD Warren Service Station 9
10	100 100 80 | 80 80 60 | 40 40 40	HOLLOWAY Nags Head 10 †
11	100 100 80 | | 60 40 40 | 40	HOLLOWAY ROAD Station 11
12	100 100 80 | 80 | 80 60 40 | 40 40	HIGHBURY & ISLINGTON Station 12 †
13	100 100 80 | | 80 60 60 | 40 40 40	ISLINGTON St. Mary's Church 13
14	150 150 110 | | 110 90 90 | 70 70 50 | 50	ANGEL Station 14
15	150 150 110 | 110 | 110 90 90 | 90 70 70 | 50 50	ST. MARKS HOSPITAL 15
16	150 150 150 | 150 | 150 110 110 | 110 110 70 | 70 50 50	OLD STREET Station 16 †
17	| | 150 110 110 | | 70 70 50 | 50	MOORGATE Finsbury Square 17
18	150 | 150 | 150 110 110 | 110 | 70 70 70 | 50 50	MOORGATE Station 18
19	| | 150 110 110 | | 70 70 70 | 50 50 50	BANK King William St (or MONUMENT N/B) 19
20	150 | 150 | 150 110 110 | 110 | 70 | 70 70 50 | 50	LONDON BRIDGE Station 20
27	--- --- --- | | 150 110 110 | | 70 70 50 | 50	SHOREDITCH CHURCH (S/B) or GT EASTERN ST Holywell La (N/B) 27
28	--- --- --- | 150 | 150 110 110 | 110 | 70 70 70 | 50 50	SHOREDITCH Commercial Street 28
29	--- --- --- | | 150 110 110 | | 70 70 70 | 70 50 50	LIVERPOOL STREET Station 29

ZONE 4(5/6) — 3 — 2 — 1

(Rev Jan 92) †-Farezone

LNT/1 [5:11:91] **43**

But one requirement, no matter how sophisticated the machine, is to carry a fare table which, if the bus is dedicated to a route, may stay permanently on board, otherwise it is collected by the driver in the morning, but I'll bet that like so many of our old running boards, they don't always get put back at night!

Special Shuttle Bus Service

Victoria Station and The Chelsea Flower Show

Fares: 70p Adults
35p Senior Citizens/ Children/ Zone 1 Travel Card Holders

LONDON GENERAL

EMPLOYMENT

In the Good Old Days when an experienced driver approached a major operator he would be 'vetted' by a guarantee company and if this was OK subject to one or more references he was in. A new starter would have to commence as a conductor and indeed many men and women were to remain so, preferring the occupation.

References were often fascinating, one man offering the local Vicar whose letter was succinct "He was married by me at St. Marys on the 20th". In another case the Laird was given as a previous employer and on being written to rang up to agree the man was excellent but had wrecked the tractor whilst drunk . . .

References from Doctors, Dominies and Postal Officials were favourites, but any ex-serviceman with a clean discharge book was regarded at least favourably.

A smaller employer probably either knew the man or woman as they could well be related, however distantly, or had known them from schooldays.

There was always a degree of interchange of staff between village bus companies with a mild degree of competition to get the most popular part-time drivers in Summer. Locally, at least, the Church sidesman, although an excellent driver came very low in public estimation, mainly as he regarded and had let known his view, that Scarborough (a favourite resort) was a den of iniquity! His miserable face was not welcomed by the girls who wanted a song on the way home.

True the Rule Book did say that passengers should not:

(xii) when in or on the vehicle to the annoyance of other persons use or operate any noisy instrument or make or combine with any other person or persons to make any excessive noise by singing shouting or otherwise;

and neither should passengers:

(xiv) throw any article from the vehicle or attach to or trail from the vehicle any streamer, balloon, flag or other article in such manner as to overhang the road:

but a sensible driver tempered his actions with the thought of a certain envelope due at the end of the journey!

Another man, the 'Gaffer' of the firm, always offered a prayer before a Sunday departure, but, then, in Malta most drivers have an enormous crucifix visible inside the vehicle . . . . . in both cases the locals regarded this as a perfectly normal foible.

But the World has changed and a few months ago a document was absent-mindedly borrowed by a driver from his Manager's desk. It related to the employment of on board staff for a new prestigious London Service and was designed to be read in conjunction with an American-planned computerised aptitude test.

RECRUITMENT

1. Vacancies should be advertised "across the board" to encourage as much interest as possible.
2. When recruiting, I would like to see transport experience INCLUDED in the advertisement. The reason for this is that when working "on board" it is not an environment that anyone "off the street" could work in straight away as possible operating problems could quickly rise. With experienced staff, the problem could be easily handled but to someone without this experience the "problem" could turn into a nightmare not only for himself but also for the customers he/she supposed to be looking after. Not exactly the image we are looking for.
3. When recruiting, anyone with anything obnoxious such as earrings, long hair or tattoos should immediately be dismissed before selection takes place. Other major items such as diction, language problems and dialect should also be taken into account.
4. Appearance, attitude and general manners need no mention here, but it goes without saying that if anyone does not IMMEDIATELY show these attributes then they are out of the running straight away.

SELECTION

1. There must be a minimum of TWO interviews. The reason for this is to:
   a) "progress" the recruitment stage.
   b) select on suitability basis - preferably with at least TWO interviewees.
   c) short list.
   d) then a second interview to determine the successful applicant.

2. After selection, the successful candidate to be trained by someone from within our organisation and NOT from the Computor/Employment Company.

3. After training there is to be a period of TWO weeks on the coaches accompanied THROUGH OUT by a Senior, Stress/Instructor to polish off what the candidate has learnt.

4. The 4 week assessment period to remain - assessed, of course, by Miss Latimer or Mrs Taylor [the employment officers].

This should, at least provide us with the guidelines we can work within.

A far cry indeed from our habit of using either the Boss's daughter, or a retired air hostess or an ex-secretary!

— The Routes, The Times and The Fares —

WHO GOES WHERE?

The study of timetables and timetabling has vexed, educated and employed numbers of brains since the earliest days of railways. Canal packet boats also had a timetable but as relatively few people possessed any form of timepiece in the early 1800s they may not have been too strict in its observance. Similarly, stage coach operators were only tight-to-time in their departures and in the time they allowed for refreshments and for ladies to "powder their noses". One of the similarities between their era and the 1950s was that the time available was rarely sufficient to visit the toilet and to eat; but one might add another similarity lay in the conditions that passengers put up with!

However, bus and coach timetabling has always been constrained by having to work within the speeds laid down in the Road Traffic Acts, local council regulations (which can include apparently irrational speed limits), traffic congestion, the availability, and hours worked, of drivers and perhaps, albeit unconsciously, one is driven by the thought that another operator a few miles away with his new vehicles can shave a few minutes from his and your previous year's timings. You must perforce gain your time-saving elsewhere, so a lunch break declines from 30 to 20 minutes. The hope of the planner is that the driver may be able to get to the cafe sooner and thus reinstate the 30 minutes, while the reality is that running time on a long journey is governed to a large extent by the driver's character and the nature of the party. As an example I can quote the London-Liverpool overnight run, prior to the building of motorways. The departure in 1951 using Crosvilles service was at 10.30 pm and the official arrival 0804. Breaks totalled one, 0517-0547 at Ternhill. However, a good driver always arrived at Stratford on Avon well before his advertised 02.29 and one could (perhaps surprisingly) get a roughish meal there, but the toilet facilities were good. At Ternhill, a half-way intelligent driver would find out where his passengers were going and assuming he had no pick-ups we could be in Liverpool by 6.30 am. The driver probably gained £2 or so in tips for this service and could, in a week, double his wages. Another, particularly Crosville-ish driver (and they could be a cranky lot) would run exactly to timetable until he met the Birkenhead-Liverpool traffic when, incredibly, he could arrive late. No tips for him, though, and precious little love for Crosville!

By 1961 (given that motorway services were in operation) it is surprising that the service still left at 10.30 pm, and arrived at 0804 precisely as before; 9 hrs 34 minutes running time.

The sadness is that a relatively short-lived company, Albatross Roadways Ltd was running a sleeper coach service in 1929, leaving at 1100 pm and requiring a mere 9 hours for the journey.

Sleep your way to London on

THE ALBATROSS SLEEPING · CAR SERVICE.

From **LIVERPOOL**

5 Commutation Row and Washington Hotel.

EVERY MONDAY, WEDNESDAY AND FRIDAY.

DEPART 11-0 p.m.

From **LONDON**

Royal Hotel, Woburn Place, Russell Square, W.C. 1.

EVERY SUNDAY, TUESDAY AND THURSDAY.

DEPART 11-0 p.m.

Single Fare 25/-

BAGGAGE LIMIT—Two Suit Cases per Passenger.

THE ALBATROSS SLEEPING CARS are designed to accommodate passengers in three cabins with four luxurious berths in each, arranged as on board Ship.

Each bunk is properly curtained off to ensure privacy and is provided with first class bedding and linen. The bunk is fitted with window and blind, electric light, clothes racks, mirror, ashtray, and bell to Steward.

There is proper lavatory and W.C. accommodation, and heating and ventilation are perfect.

The Steward is entirely at the service of passengers and will attend to all requirements at any time during the journey.

Tea or coffee and biscuits are served in the early morning Free of Charge. Boots are cleaned, and clothes brushed by request.

The vehicles are equipped with 6-cylinder Sleeve Valve Daimler Engines and Servo operated four wheel brakes, etc., etc.

During the 1950s peak season various other operators obtained licences for this route and at night the confusion at Victoria Coach Station was horrendous. In those days, too, a serviceman was required to wear his uniform and indeed most personnel were proud to do so. A Standerwick relief driver, finding there were half a dozen uniformed men on board, all going to visit their wives or girl friends drove his ECW-bodied Bristol hard through the night and despite giving us 2 half hour breaks still arrived at a rainswept Liverpool by 0513. Fortunately, most of the women were waiting as apparently they knew the habits of Standerwick drivers!

This then was an express service, to all intents and purposes unchanged for thirty years.

The great competitive days were in the early 1930s when entrepreneurial types thought they could take on the big boys and if not beat them at least carve a niche for themselves. Realistically, they really had little chance as the major companies had been, or were to be, bought up by the railway companies. This is not to say that these larger companies could be complacent but with

IMPORTANT.

This ticket entitles the holder, if desired, to make the return journey by Rail to Liverpool Street Station by any train upon payment at the appropriate Railway Station booking office of a supplement per passenger as under:—

	Norwich (Thorps)	Yarmouth (South Town)
Day Return	**3/-**	—
Period	**4/-**	**4/6**

their buying power, ordering perhaps twenty or thirty chassis at a time, they could undercut the independants prime vehicle costs and with the life of front line coaches only being three years the smaller concerns could neither depreciate their vehicles and still show a profit nor pass them on to a subsidiary for secondary use. Rightly or wrongly, the Traffic Commissioners tended to favour larger companies when applications were made for extra services as the Commissioners believed they had the vehicles and manpower to provide back-up in the event of breakdowns or other untoward circumstances. Not entirely surprisingly, history is repeating itself today as many of the bright new post-regulation companies either go to the wall or are glad to be bought out by the big-money operators.

Even during the earliest years of bus operation there were examples of co-ordinated services, where one feels both parties were getting exhausted with the battle. In this particular case the result later followed the usual pattern as the Lancaster & District Tramways Company never electrified their line and changed to being a bus operator in 1921, subsequently being acquired by Fahy's; themselves later a subsidiary of Ribble. A curiosity of their timetable though is the paragraph commencing with "N.B." This must surely have been written by a Fahy!

Lancaster & District Tramways Co., Ltd.
And Fahys, Ltd.

MOTOR OMNIBUS SERVICE

— **BETWEEN** —

Lancaster & Morecambe.

Time Table

Commencing MONDAY, April 20th, 1914,

And until further notice.

Leave MORECAMBE (Market Street).

MORNING ; *9-10, 9-40, 10-10, 10-40, 11-10, 11-40.

AFTERNOON : 12-10, *12-40, *1-10, *1-40,2-10, 2-40, 3-10, 3-40, 4-10, *4-40, 5-10, 5-40, 6-10, *6-40, 7-10, 7-40, 8-10, 8-40, 9-10, 9-40, 10-10, 10-40.

Leave LANCASTER (Stonewell).

MORNING : 9-40, 10-10, 10-40, 11-10, 11-40.

AFTERNOON ; *12.10, 12-40, *1-10, 1-40, 2-10, 2-40, 3-10, 3-40 *4-10, 4-40, *5-10, *5-40, 6-10, 6-40, 7-10, 7-40, 8-10, 8-40, *9-10, 9-40, 10-10, 10-40, *11-10.

N.B.—To meet the convenience of people residing at Skerton, the Buses marked thus * will run via Lune Villa Lodge. This will be in place of the Motor Char-a-Banc now running to Skerton, which ceased on Tuesday, April 7th.

— **SUNDAYS.** —

LEAVE MORECAMBE.

AFTERNOON : 12-10, and every half-hour until **10-10 p.m.**

LEAVE LANCASTER.

AFTERNOON : 12-40, and every half-hour until **10-40 p.m.**

Still in the 1930s it was the practice of many operators to issue really quite large, but not always informative, leaflets. Photographs of early booking agencies show how blackboards, posters and racks of leaflets all jostled for the passer-by's attention.

Commencing Monday, December 1st, 1930, a Fast, Frequent Service of Saloon Coaches will operate

between

UPMINSTER & LONDON
(ALDGATE)

via

Hornchurch, Becontree Heath, Green Lane (Goodmayes), Ilford Broadway, Stratford, Bow, Mile End, Aldgate.

A handy Pocket Time Table, giving particulars of Times of Departures, Workmen's, Cheap Mid-day and Season Tickets, etc., may be obtained from any of the following Agents, or Company's Office.

UPMINSTER GARAGE, UPMINSTER
THE CORNER SHOP, 197, RUSH GREEN ROAD, ROMFORD
MAYFIELD MOTORS,
660, GREEN LANE, GOODMAYES, ILFORD

All Coaches will stop if you hail them

Head Office—
28/30, CHAPEL STREET, STRATFORD, E.15.
Telephone: Maryland 2037 & 3634

CLARK, ILFORD.

Woodgrange Coaches' leaflet was not really the most helpful as they only advised the public that they would offer a "Fast Frequent Service" and the would-be user had to go to the bother of another visit to one of three agents. Why not at least add some times? It is not really much use to state "All Coaches will stop if you hail them" when the would-be passenger knows neither time nor route!

◄ Their route was later to be superceded by the Green Line 722 service from Corbets Tye to Aldgate.

Another, only slightly more informative paper came from an information bureau in September 1928 and is interesting in that this was a very early date for through London-Glasgow Services. A year later Thomson's, whose head office was in Hope Street, Glasgow, were offering an Edinburgh-Glasgow-London service thrice weekly, while another firm, Clan Motorways offered to carry passengers from London (dep 8 a.m.) via Glasgow (arr 7 a.m./dep 1000 a.m.) to Aberdeen, where the battered, dazed body was deposited at 5.10 p.m. Apart from the low price it is difficult to see anything to commend in a journey of this type unless one over-nighted en route. ▼

9 ST. JOHN'S LANE. Sept, 1928
31 OLD HAYMARKET

IMPERIAL MOTORWAYS

Booking Offices & Waiting Rooms
5 Commutation Row
AND
35 Carlton Pl., Glasgow
Telephones—
North 115, Waterloo 719.
Glasgow, South 983.

LUXURIOUS
Saloon Coach Service
BETWEEN
LIVERPOOL
AND
GLASGOW
Single 20s. Return-36s

Preston, Penrith
Garstang, Carlisle
Lancaster, Dumfries
Kendal, Kilmarnock
Shap

These Coaches leave Liverpool daily at 9 a.m. prompt from **5 COMMUTATION ROW.**

Coach leaves Glasgow daily at 9 a.m. from **BUS INFORMATION BUREAU, 85 Carlton Place.**

SUNDAYS — Coaches leave all Stages half an hour later.

Glasgow Booking Office:
Bus Information Bureau, 85 CARLTON PLACE
Telephone—South 983.

Bus Information and Motor Tours Bureau

MOTOR COACH TOURS

Not to One Place only in **SCOTLAND** but **ALL OVER** in
DE LUXE TOURING COACHES

Chief Organiser for Scotland—
ANDREW J. THOMSON

Daily Omnibus Services to—
AYR
ABERDEEN
ARDROSSAN
BALLANTRAE
DUNDEE
GIRVAN
GOUROCK
LARGS
LIVERPOOL
LONDON
MANCHESTER
NEWCASTLE
OBAN
PEEBLES
STIRLING
TROON
WHITLEY BAY

A News Reel in the Original

85 CARLTON PL.
GLASGOW, C.5
Telephone—South 983.

Booking Agent and Enquiry Office representing all the Leading Bus Services and Motor Tours in Scotland, England, Ireland and Wales.

Private Parties Booked.

Parcels and Left Luggage Office.

SPECIAL TOURS
Oban and Western Highlands, Loch Lomond and Trossachs, The Burns Country, The Three Lochs, Trossachs, Braemar, Dryburgh and Melrose Abbeys, Pass of Killiecrankie, Pass of Glencoe, Inveraray and Dalmally, Inverness 3 days' tour, Blackpool 4 days' tour. English Lakes, do. Isle of Skye 5 days' tour, Highland Tour, 5 and 8 days' tour, Devon and Cornwall 8 and 14 days' tour.

COUNTY Motor Services

STAKEFORD, CHOPPINGTON, NORTHUMBERLAND and
Bus Information Bureau
85 Carlton Place.
Glasgow, C.5.
Telephones—
Ashington 108; South 983.

DAILY
Saloon Coach Service
BETWEEN
GLASGOW
EDINBURGH, KELSO, COLDSTREAM NEWCASTLE WHITLEY BAY and
LONDON

	Single £ s. d.	Return £ s. d.
Glasgow to London	1 13 0	2 18 0
Glasgow to Whitley Bay	0 13 8	1 4 0
Glasgow to Newcastle	0 13 0	1 3 0
Edinburgh to Whitley Bay	0 11 4	0 18 6
Edinburgh to Newcastle ..	0 10 6	0 17 6

Pioneers o fthe Glasgow, Edinburgh, Newcastle, Whitley Bay and London Services.

Glasgow Booking Office:
Bus Information Bureau, 85 CARLTON PLACE
Telephone—South 983.

- TIME TABLE -

GLASGOW Southward Journey

		p.m.
Glasgow (Buchanan St. Bus Station)...	depart	7 00
Hamilton (Excelsior Agency, New Cross)	„	7 30
Gretna (Union Jack Hotel)	„	10 18
Carlisle (Blair & Palmers' Garage) ...	„	10 35
Carlisle (Bus Station, Lowther Street and Country Cafe)	arrive	10 38
Carlisle (Bus Station, Lowther Street) ...	depart	10 58
Penrith (Crown Hotel)	„	11 43
		a.m.
Boroughbridge (Kelly's Cafe)	„	2 33
Doncaster (Fisher's Cafe)	„	4 13
Grantham (Lymes Cafe)...	arrive	6 08
Grantham (Lymes Cafe)...	depart	6 28
Grantham (Post Office)	„	6 32
Stamford (Square)	„	7 11
Baldock (Alnott's Cafe)	„	9 13
London (Victoria Coach Station)	...arr. abt.	10 54

LONDON Northward Journey

		p.m.
London (Victoria Coach Station)	. depart	8 00
Baldock (Alnott's Cafe)	„	9 41
Stamford (Square)	„	11 43
		a.m.
Grantham (Post Office)	„	12 21
Grantham (Lymes Cafe)...	arrive	12 26
Grantham (Lymes Cafe)...	depart	12 46
Doncaster (Fisher's Cafe)	„	2 41
Boroughbridge (Kelly's Cafe)	„	3 21
Penrith (Crown Hotel)	„	7 11
Carlisle (Bus Station, Lowther Street and Country Cafe)	arrive	7 56
Carlisle (Bus Station, Lowther Street) ...	depart	8 16
Carlisle (Blair & Palmers' Garage) ...	„	8 19
Gretna (Union Jack Hotel)	„	8 36
Hamilton (Excelsior Agency, New Cross)	depart	11 24
Glasgow (Buchanan St. Bus Station)..	.arr. abt.	11 54

FARES *(Principal Fares)* LIST

	Single	Return
Glasgow - Boroughbridge ...	18/-	
Glasgow—Doncaster ...	21/-	40/-
Glasgow—Grantham ...	26/-	43/-
Glasgow - London ...	30/-	50/-

	Single	Return
London - Carlisle ...	27/-	45/-
London—Penrith ...	26/-	43/-
London—Lockerbie ...	30/-	50/-

CHILDREN over 3 and under 14 years of age—Half of Adult Fare to nearest threepence.

CONDITIONS

BOOKINGS:—Passengers on Booking Return Tickets must apply at the same time for seat reservation for the Return Journey.

LUGGAGE:—Passengers allowed 40 lbs. personal luggage free, limited in size to 26 in. x 18 in. x 12 in. The Company do not hold themselves responsible for loss or damage to any kind of luggage. Passengers are recommended to insure luggage.

▲

The Western SMT timetable was probably for the Coronation year 1937 when the fare had been reduced by 5/- (25p or 15%) and the journey was down to nearly half the running time. This latter timetable is clear, informative and very professional.

In the halcyon days of flying when there was some degree of excitement to be found even in a simple journey, passengers understood that there was a good chance that they would commence or finish the journey by coach, a fact borne out by this timetable which appears to suggest an element of road carriage, presumably normally from London to Croydon or to Paris from Le Bourget. ➤

IMPERIAL AIRWAYS

THE ONLY BRITISH AIRLINE to the CONTINENT

Through Bookings, Motor Coach and Air, from

THE CENTRAL LONDON STATION

Museum 8331—9 Crescent Place, Cartwright Gardens, W.C.1

SUMMER TIME TABLE

LONDON—PARIS—BASLE

	A			A
From **LONDON**	a.m.	a.m.	a.m.	p.m.
Airways House	7.15	9.40	11.10	3.40
Croydon	8.0	10.30	12.0	4.30
		p.m.	p.m.	
Arr. **PARIS** (Le Bourget)	10.30	1.0	2.30	7.20
Dep. **PARIS** (Le Bourget)	—	2.0	—	—
Arr. **BASLE** (Birsfelden Aerodrome)	—	5.0	—	—
Dep. **BASLE**	—	5.30	—	—
Arr. **ZURICH**	—	6.15	—	—
		a.m.		
Dep. **ZURICH**	—	8.15	—	—
Arr. **BASLE**	—	9.0	—	—
Dep. **BASLE**	—	9.30	—	—
Arr. **PARIS** (Le Bourget)	—	12.45	—	—
		p.m.		p.m.
Dep. **PARIS** (Le Bourget)	8.0	2.15	noon	4.0
			p.m.	
Arr. **CROYDON**	10.50	4.45	2.30	6.30

A—Not Sunday.

LONDON—BRUSSELS—COLOGNE *(Sunday excepted)*

From **LONDON**	a.m.
Airways House	8.10
Croydon Aerodrome	9.0
Arr. **BRUSSELS** (Haren Aerodrome)	11.30
Dep. **HAREN AERODROME** ..	11.30
	p.m.
Arr. **COLOGNE** (Bickendorf Aerodrome)	2.0*

From **COLOGNE**	p.m.
(Bickendorf Aerodrome) ..	2.15*
Arr. **BRUSSELS** (Haren Aerodrome)	4.30
Dep. **HAREN AERODROME**..	5.0
Arr. **CROYDON**	7.40

* Mid-European time.

NOTE.—Connections in Cologne for Deutsche-Luft-Hansa services.

Fares.	Sgl.	Rtn.
London–Paris	£4 15 0	£9 0 0
London–Paris (Silver-Wing, i.e., midday plane) ..	£5 15 0	£10 18 6
London–Brussels	£5 0 0	£9 10 0
London–Basle	£7 10 0	£14 5 0
London–Cologne	£5 15 0	£10 18 6
London–Zurich	£8 5 0	£15 13 6

IMPERIAL AIRWAYS

THE STRAIGHT LINE WAY

TIME TABLES

SERVICE No. 2.

Cardiff—Lampeter—Aberystwyth via Aberdare.

Cardiff	7.45 a.m.	Aberystwyth	4.30 p.m.
Pontypridd	8.21 „	Aberayron	5.18 „
Abercynon	8.30 „	Lampeter	5.37 „
Mountain Ash	8.42 „	Llandilo	6.57 „
Aberdare	8.54 „	Ammanford	7.22 „
Hirwaun	9.3 „	Pontardawe	7.52 „
Glyn Neath	9.15 „	Clydach	8.2 „
Resolven	9.33 „	Skewen	8.15 „
Aberdulais	9.45 „	Neath	8.22 „
Neath	9.51 „	Aberdulais	8.28 „
Skewen	10.0 „	Resolven	8.40 „
Clydach	10.12 „	Glyn Neath	8.58 „
Pontardawe	10.21 „	Hirwaun	9.10 „
Ammanford	10.51 „	Aberdare	9.19 „
Llandilo	11.16 „	Mountain Ash	9.31 „
Lampeter	12.16 p.m.	Abercynon	9.43 „
Aberayron	12.55 „	Pontypridd	9.52 „
Aberystwyth	1.43 „	Cardiff	10.30 „

SERVICE No. 3.

Cardiff—Lampeter—Aberystwyth via Tonypandy.

Cardiff	7.0 a.m.	Aberystwyth	4.30 p.m.
Llandaff	7.5 „	Aberayron	5.18 „
Miskin	7.25 „	Lampeter	5.37 „
Pontyclun	7.27 „	Llandilo	6.57 „
Talbot	7.29 „	Ammanford	7.22 „
Tonyrefail	7.40 „	Pontardawe	7.52 „
Penygraig	7.55 „	Clydach	8.2 „
Tonypandy	7.58 „	Skewen	8.15 „
Ystrad	8.9 „	Neath	8.22 „
Pentre	8.13 „	Aberdulais	8.28 „
Treorchy	8.16 „	Resolven	8.40 „
Treherbert	8.20 „	Glyn Neath	8.58 „
Glyn Neath	9.15 „	Treherbert	9.52 „
Resolven	9.33 „	Treorchy	9.56 „
Aberdulais	9.45 „	Pentre	9.59 „
Neath	9.51 „	Ystrad	10.3 „
Skewen	10.0 „	Tonypandy	10.14 „
Clydach	10.12 „	Penygraig	10.17 „
Pontardawe	10.21 „	Tonyrefail	10.32 „
Ammanford	10.51 „	Talbot	10.43 „
Llandilo	11.16 „	Pontyclun	10.45 „
Lampeter	12.16 p.m.	Miskin	10.47 „
Aberayron	12.55 „	Llandaff	11.7 „
Aberystwyth	1.43 „	Cardiff	11.12 „

SERVICE No. 4.

Cardiff—Lampeter—Aberystwyth via Porth.

Cardiff	7.20 a.m.	Aberystwyth	4.30 p.m.
Pontypridd	7.40 „	Aberayron	5.18 „
Trehafod	7.46 „	Lampeter	5.37 „
Porth	7.55 „	Llandilo	6.57 „
Ynyshir	8.0 „	Ammanford	7.22 „
Pontygwaith	8.5 „	Pontardawe	7.52 „
Tylorstown	8.10 „	Clydach	8.2 „
Ferndale	8.15 „	Skewen	8.15 „
Mardy	8.23 „	Neath	8.22 „
Aberdare	8.54 „	Aberdulais	8.28 „
Hirwaun	9.3 „	Resolven	8.40 „
Glyn Neath	9.15 „	Glyn Neath	8.58 „
Resolven	9.33 „	Hirwaun	9.10 „
Aberdulais	9.45 „	Aberdare	9.19 „
Neath	9.51 „	Mardy	9.50 „
Skewen	10.0 „	Ferndale	9.58 „
Clydach	10.12 „	Tylorstown	10.3 „
Pontardawe	10.21 „	Pontygwaith	10.8 „
Ammanford	10.51 „	Ynyshir	10.13 „
Llandilo	11.16 „	Porth	10.18 „
Lampeter	12.16 p.m.	Trehafod	10.27 „
Aberayron	12.55 „	Pontypridd	10.33 „
Aberystwyth	1.43 „	Cardiff	10.53 „

SERVICE No. 6.

Cardiff—Cardigan—Aberystwyth via Aberdare.

Cardiff	7.45 a.m.	Aberystwyth	2.30 p.m.
Pontypridd	8.21 „	Aberayron	3.33 „
Abercynon	8.30 „	Synod (New Quay)	3.57 „
Mountain Ash	8.42 „	Gogerddan (Aberporth	4.27 „
Aberdare	8.54 „	Cardigan	4.45 „
Hirwaun	9.3 „	Newcastle Emlyn	5.15 „
Glyn Neath	9.15 „	Carmarthen	6.15 „
Resolven	9.33 „	Kidwelly	6.51 „
Aberdulais	9.45 „	Pembrey	7.3 „
Neath	9.51 „	Burry Port	7.6 „
Skewen	10.0 „	Llanelly	7.15 „
Swansea	10.20 „	Lougher	7.28 „
Gorseinon	10.41 „	Gorseinon	7.34 „
Lougher	10.47 „	Swansea	7.55 „
Llanelly	11.0 „	Skewen	8.15 „
Burry Port	11.9 „	Neath	8.22 „
Pembrey	11.12 „	Aberdulais	8.28 „
Kidwelly	11.24 „	Resolven	8.40 „
Carmarthen	12.0 noon	Glyn Neath	8.58 „
Newcastle Emlyn	1.0 p.m.	Hirwaun	9.10 „
Cardigan	1.30 „	Aberdare	9.19 „
Gogerddan (Aberporth)	1.50 „	Mountain Ash	9.31 „
Synod (New Quay)	2.20 „	Abercynon	9.43 „
Aberayron	2.44 „	Pontypridd	9.52 „
Aberystwyth	3.45 „	Cardiff	10.30 „

SERVICE No. 7.

Cardiff—Cardigan—Aberystwyth via Tonypandy.

Cardiff	7.0 a.m.	Aberystwyth	2.30 p.m.
Llandaff	7.5 „	Aberayron	3.33 „
Miskin	7.25 „	Synod (New Quay)	3.57 „
Pontyclun	7.27 „	Gogerddan (Aberporth)	4.27 „
Talbot	7.29 „	Cardigan	4.45 „
Tonyrefail	7.40 „	Newcastle Emlyn	5.15 „
Penygraig	7.55 „	Carmarthen	6.15 „
Tonypandy	7.58 „	Kidwelly	6.51 „
Ystrad	8.9 „	Pembrey	7.3 „
Pentre	8.13 „	Burry Port	7.6 „
Treorchy	8.16 „	Llanelly	7.15 „
Treherbert	8.20 „	Lougher	7.28 „
Glyn Neath	9.15 „	Gorseinon	7.34 „
Resolven	9.33 „	Swansea	7.55 „
Aberdulais	9.45 .	Skewen	8.15 „
Neath	9.51 „	Neath	8.22 „
Skewen	10.0 „	Aberdulais	8.28 „
Swansea	10.20 „	Resolven	8.40 „
Gorseinon	10.41 „	Glyn Neath	8.58 „
Lougher	10.47 „	Treherbert	9.52 „
Llanelly	11.0 „	Treorchy	9.56 „
Burry Port	11.9 „	Pentre	9.59 „
Pembrey	11.12 „	Ystrad	10.3 „
Kidwelly	11.24 „	Tonypandy	10.14 „
Carmarthen	12.0 noon	Penygraig	10.17 „
Newcastle Emlyn	1.0 p.m.	Tonyrefail	10.32 „
Cardigan	1.30 „	Talbot	10.43 „
Gogerddan (Aberporth)	1.50 „	Pontyclun	10.45 „
Synod (New Quay)	2.20 „	Miskin	10.47 „
Aberayron	2.44 „	Llandaff	11.7 „
Aberystwyth	3.45 „	Cardiff	11.12 „

SERVICE No. 8.

Cardiff—Cardigan—Aberystwyth via Porth.

Cardiff	7.20 a.m.	Aberystwyth	2.30 p.m.
Pontypridd	7.40 „	Aberayron	3.33 „
Trehafod	7.46 „	Synod (New Quay)	3.57 „
Porth	7.55 „	Gogerddan (Aberporth)	4.27 „
Ynyshir	8.0 „	Cardigan	4.45 „
Pontygwaith	8.5 „	Newcastle Emlyn	5.15 „
Tylorstown	8.10 „	Carmarthen	6.15 „
Ferndale	8.15 „	Kidwelly	6.51 „
Mardy	8.23 „	Pembrey	7.3 „
Aberdare	8.54 „	Burry Port	7.6 „
Hirwaun	9.3 „	Llanelly	7.15 „
Glyn Neath	9.15 „	Lougher	7.28 „
Resolven	9.33 „	Gorseinon	7.34 „
Aberdulais	9.45 „	Swansea	7.55 „
Neath	9.51 „	Skewen	8.15 „
Skewen	10.0 „	Neath	8.22 „
Swansea	10.20 „	Aberdulais	8.28 „
Gorseinon	10.41 „	Resolven	8.40 „
Lougher	10.47 „	Glyn Neath	8.58 „
Llanelly	11.0 „	Hirwaun	9.10 „
Burry Port	11.9 „	Aberdare	9.19 „
Pembrey	11.12 „	Mardy	9.50 „
Kidwelly	11.24 „	Ferndale	9.58 „
Carmarthen	12.0 noon	Tylorstown	10.3 „
Newcastle Emlyn	1.0 p.m.	Pontygwaith	10.8 „
Cardigan	1.30 „	Ynyshir	10.13 „
Gogerddan (Aberporth)	1.50 „	Porth	10.18 „
Synod (New Quay)	2.20 „	Trehafod	10.27 „
Aberayron	2.44 „	Pontypridd	10.33 „
Aberystwyth	3.45 „	Cardiff	10.53 „

All seats must be booked at least 48 hours in advance and return date must be stated at time of booking.

Daily Service from SOUTH WALES to CARDIGAN and ABERYSTWYTH, Etc.

BOOKING AGENTS IN EVERY TOWN.

LOCAL AGENT :

HEAD OFFICES :

GOUGH'S WELSH MOTORWAYS Ltd.

Auto House, MOUNTAIN ASH. Phone 22.

Maindy Depot, CARDIFF. Phone 2196.

One approach by an operator keen on catching the public's eye was to show a racy drawing of their latest vehicle on the front of their leaflet or timetable, this (rather battered) document was issued in the late-1930s and covered all Gough's main services. The cover and part of a time-table are reproduced.

Gough's of Mountain Ash were one of the oldest firms to operate in Wales, claiming to have run a char-a-banc before World War I. They were to sell out to Red & White in 1936, by which time they owned 37 vehicles.

Current 1935

WHITE'S MOTORS.

ROUTE 4.

FERNDALE, TYLORSTOWN, PORTH, PONTYPRIDD, AND CARDIFF.

CARDIFF—PONTYPRIDD Section, Operated Jointly by White's Motors, Western Welsh, and Rhondda Tramways, Ltd.
CARDIFF, PORTH, FERNDALE SECTION, Operated Jointly by White's Motors and Rhondda Tramways, Ltd.

JOINT TIME TABLE.

WEEK-DAYS.

	a.m.	a.m.	a.m.	a.m.	a.m.	a.m.	a.m.	a.m.	a.m.	a.m.	a.m.	a.m.	a.m.	a.m.	a.m.	a.m.	a.m.	a.m.	a.m.	a.m.	a.m.	p.m.	p.m.	
FERNDALE (Strand)	..	..	7 30	..	..	..	8 30	..	..	..	9 30	..	..	..	10 30	..	..	..	..	..	11 30	..	..	And similar Intervals until
Tylorstown (Queen's Square)	..	..	7 34	..	..	..	8 35	..	..	..	9 35	..	..	..	10 35	..	..	..	..	..	11 35	..	..	
Wattstown	..	..	7 40	..	..	..	8 40	..	..	..	9 40	..	..	..	10 40	..	..	..	..	..	11 40	..	..	
PORTH (Station Square)	7 0	..	7 48	..	..	..	8 48	..	..	..	9 48	..	..	..	10 48	..	..	..	..	..	11 48	..	..	
Trehafod	7 4	..	7 52	..	..	..	8 52	..	..	..	9 52	..	..	..	10 52	..	..	..	..	..	11 52	..	..	
PONTYPRIDD (New Inn)	7 12	..	8 0	..	..	..	9 0	..	..	..	10 0	..	..	..	11 0	..	..	..	..	..	12 0	..	..	
do. (Queen's Hotel)	7 15	..	8 5	..	..	..	9 5	..	..	..	10 5	..	..	..	11 5	..	..	..	..	..	12 5	..	..	
do. (Station Square)	—	7 55	—	8 20	8 35	8 50	—	9 20	9 35	9 50	—	10 20	10 35	10 50	—	11 15	11 25	11 35	11 45	11 55	—	12 15	12 25	
Glyntaff	7 18	8 0	8 9	8 24	8 39	8 54	9 9	9 24	9 39	9 54	10 9	10 24	10 39	10 54	11 9	11 19	11 29	11 39	11 49	11 59	12 9	12 19	12 29	
Rhydyfelin Station	7 20	8 2	8 12	8 27	8 42	8 57	9 12	9 27	9 42	9 57	10 12	10 27	10 42	10 57	11 12	11 22	11 32	11 42	11 52	12 2	12 12	12 22	12 32	
Upper Boat	7 24	8 6	8 16	8 31	8 46	9 1	9 16	9 31	9 46	10 1	10 16	10 31	10 46	11 1	11 16	11 26	11 36	11 46	11 56	12 6	12 16	12 26	12 36	
Nantgarw	7 28	8 11	8 21	8 36	8 51	9 6	9 21	9 36	9 51	10 6	10 21	10 36	10 51	11 6	11 21	11 31	11 41	11 51	12 1	12 11	12 21	12 31	12 41	
Taffs Well P.O.	7 33	8 16	8 26	8 41	8 56	9 11	9 26	9 41	9 56	10 11	10 26	10 41	10 56	11 11	11 26	11 36	11 46	11 56	12 6	12 16	12 26	12 36	12 46	
Tongwynlais	7 36	8 19	8 29	8 44	8 59	9 14	9 29	9 44	9 59	10 14	10 29	10 44	10 59	11 14	11 29	11 39	11 49	11 59	12 9	12 19	12 29	12 39	12 49	
Holly Bush	7 40	8 23	8 33	8 48	9 3	9 18	9 33	9 48	10 3	10 18	10 33	10 48	11 3	11 18	11 33	11 43	11 53	12 3	12 13	12 23	12 33	12 43	12 53	
Whitchurch (Library)	7 42	8 25	8 35	8 50	9 5	9 20	9 35	9 50	10 5	10 20	10 35	10 50	11 5	11 20	11 35	11 45	11 55	12 5	12 15	12 25	12 35	12 45	12 55	
CARDIFF (Park Place)	7 54	8 37	8 47	9 2	9 17	9 32	9 47	10 2	10 17	10 32	10 47	11 2	11 17	11 32	11 47	11 57	12 7	12 17	12 27	12 37	12 47	12 57	1 7	

	WEEK-DAYS—continued.					SUNDAYS.																	
	p.m.	p.m.	p.m.	p.m.	p.m.	a.m.	a.m.	a.m.	a.m.	a.m.	a.m.	a.m.	a.m.	a.m.	a.m.	a.m.	p.m.		p.m.	p.m.	p.m.	p.m.	p.m.
FERNDALE (Strand)	..	10 30	..	..	..	..	..	9 30	..	..	10 30	..	..	..	11 30	..	..	And similar Intervals until	..	..	..	10 30	..
Tylorstown (Queen's Square)	..	10 35	..	..	..	..	..	9 35	..	..	10 35	..	..	..	11 35	..	..		..	..	..	10 35	..
Wattstown	..	10 40	..	..	..	..	..	9 40	..	..	10 40	..	..	..	11 40	..	..		..	..	..	10 40	..
PORTH (Station Square)	..	10 48	..	..	..	8 48	..	9 48	..	..	10 48	..	..	..	11 48	..	..		..	..	..	10 48	..
Trehafod	..	10 52	..	..	..	8 52	..	9 52	..	..	10 52	..	..	..	11 52	..	..		..	..	..	10 52	..
PONTYPRIDD (New Inn)	..	11 0	..	..	..	9 0	..	10 0	..	..	11 0	..	..	..	12 0	..	..		..	..	..	11 0	..
do. (Queen's Hotel)	..	11 5	..	..	..	9 5	..	10 5	..	..	11 5	..	..	..	12 5	..	..		..	..	..	11 5	..
do. (Station Square)	10 55	—	11 15	11 25	11 35	—	9 35	—	10 35	10 50	—	11 20	11 35	11 50	—	12 20	12 35		10 20	10 35	10 50	—	11 15
Glyntaff	10 59	11 9	11 19	11 29	11 39	9 9	9 39	10 9	10 39	10 54	11 9	11 24	11 39	11 54	12 9	12 24	12 39		10 24	10 39	10 54	11 9	11 19
Rhydyfelin Station	11 2	11 12	11 22	11 32	11 42	9 12	9 42	10 12	10 42	10 57	11 12	11 27	11 42	11 57	12 12	12 27	12 42		10 27	10 42	10 57	11 12	11 22
Upper Boat	11 6	11 16	11 26	11 36	11 46	9 16	9 46	10 16	10 46	11 1	11 16	11 31	11 46	12 1	12 16	12 31	12 46		10 31	10 46	11 1	11 16	11 26
Nantgarw	11 11	11 21	11 31	11 41	11 51	9 21	9 51	10 21	10 51	11 6	11 21	11 36	11 51	12 6	12 21	12 36	12 51		10 36	10 51	11 6	11 21	11 31
Taffs Well P.O.	11 16	11 26	11 36	11 46	11 56	9 26	9 56	10 26	10 56	11 11	11 26	11 41	11 56	12 11	12 26	12 41	12 56		10 41	10 56	11 11	11 26	11 36
Tongwynlais	11 19	11 29	11 39	11 49	11 59	9 29	9 59	10 29	10 59	11 14	11 29	11 44	11 59	12 14	12 29	12 44	12 59		10 44	10 59	11 14	11 29	11 39
Holly Bush	11 23	11 33	11 43	11 53	12 3	9 33	10 3	10 33	11 3	11 18	11 33	11 48	12 3	12 18	12 33	12 48	1 3		10 48	11 3	11 18	11 33	11 43
Whitchurch (Library)	11 25	11 35	11 45	11 55	12 5	9 35	10 5	10 35	11 5	11 20	11 35	11 50	12 5	12 20	12 35	12 50	1 5		10 50	11 5	11 20	11 35	11 45
CARDIFF (Park Place)	11 37	11 47	11 57	12 7	12 17	9 47	10 17	10 47	11 17	11 32	11 47	12 2	12 17	12 32	12 47	1 2	1 17		11 2	11 17	11 32	11 47	11 57

WEEK-DAYS.

	a.m.	a.m.	a.m.	a.m.	a.m.	a.m.	a.m.	a.m.	a.m.	a.m.	a.m.	a.m.	a.m.	a.m.	a.m.	a.m.	a.m.	a.m.	a.m.	a.m.	a.m.	a.m.	noon	
CARDIFF (Park Place)	6 10	7 20	7 40	8 0	8 15	8 30	8 45	9 0	9 15	9 30	9 45	10 0	10 15	10 30	10 40	10 50	11 0	11 10	11 20	11 30	11 40	11 50	12 0	And similar Intervals until
Whitchurch (Library)	6 22	7 32	7 52	8 12	8 27	8 42	8 57	9 12	9 27	9 42	9 57	10 12	10 27	10 42	10 52	11 2	11 12	11 22	11 32	11 42	11 52	12 2	12 12	
Holly Bush	6 24	7 34	7 54	8 14	8 29	8 44	8 59	9 14	9 29	9 44	9 59	10 14	10 29	10 44	10 54	11 4	11 14	11 24	11 34	11 44	11 54	12 4	12 14	
Tongwynlais	6 27	7 37	7 57	8 17	8 32	8 47	9 2	9 17	9 32	9 47	10 2	10 17	10 32	10 47	10 57	11 7	11 17	11 27	11 37	11 47	11 57	12 7	12 17	
Taffs Well P.O.	6 31	7 41	8 1	8 21	8 36	8 51	9 6	9 21	9 36	9 51	10 6	10 21	10 36	10 51	11 1	11 11	11 21	11 31	11 41	11 51	12 1	12 11	12 21	
Nantgarw	6 36	7 46	8 6	8 26	8 41	8 56	9 11	9 26	9 41	9 56	10 11	10 26	10 41	10 56	11 6	11 16	11 26	11 36	11 46	11 56	12 6	12 16	12 26	
Upper Boat	6 40	7 50	8 10	8 30	8 45	9 0	9 15	9 30	9 45	10 0	10 15	10 30	10 45	11 0	11 10	11 20	11 30	11 40	11 50	12 0	12 10	12 20	12 30	
Rhydyfelin Station	6 44	7 56	8 16	8 34	8 51	9 6	9 21	9 36	9 51	10 6	10 21	10 36	10 51	11 6	11 16	11 26	11 36	11 46	11 56	12 6	12 16	12 26	12 36	
Glyntaff	6 46	7 58	8 18	8 36	8 53	9 8	9 23	9 38	9 53	10 8	10 23	10 38	10 53	11 8	11 18	11 28	11 38	11 48	11 58	12 8	12 18	12 28	12 38	
PONTYPRIDD (Station Square)	—	8 3	8 23	—	8 58	9 13	9 28	—	9 58	10 13	10 28	—	10 58	11 13	11 23	11 33	—	11 53	12 8	12 13	12 23	12 33		
do. (Queen's Hotel)	6 50	..	..	8 40	..	..	..	9 45	..	..	..	10 45	..	..	..	..	11 45	..	..	..	..	..	12 45	
do. (New Inn)	6 52	..	..	8 42	..	..	..	9 47	..	..	..	10 47	..	..	..	..	11 47	..	..	..	..	..	12 47	
Trehafod	7 0	..	..	8 50	..	..	..	9 55	..	..	..	10 55	..	..	..	..	11 55	..	..	..	..	..	12 55	
PORTH (Station Square)	7 5	..	..	8 55	..	..	..	10 0	..	..	..	11 0	..	..	..	..	12 0	..	..	..	..	..	1 0	
Wattstown	7 13	..	..	9 3	..	..	..	10 8	..	..	..	11 8	..	..	..	..	12 8	..	..	..	..	..	1 8	
Tylorstown (Queen's Square)	7 20	..	..	9 10	..	..	..	10 15	..	..	..	11 15	..	..	..	..	12 15	..	..	..	..	..	1 15	
FERNDALE (Strand)	7 25	..	..	9 15	..	..	..	10 20	..	..	..	11 20	..	..	..	..	12 20	..	..	..	..	..	1 20	

	WEEK-DAYS—continued.								SUNDAYS.														
	p.m.	p.m.	p.m.	p.m.	p.m.	p.m.	p.m.	p.m.	a.m.	a.m.	a.m.	a.m.	a.m.	a.m.	a.m.	a.m.	a.m.		p.m.	p.m.	p.m.	p.m.	p.m.
CARDIFF (Park Place)	10 0	10 10	10 20	10 30	10 40	10 50	11 5	11 15	9 0	9 30	9 45	10 0	10 15	10 30	11 0	11 15	11 30	similar Intervals until	10 0	10 15	10 30	10 50	11 5
Whitchurch (Library)	10 12	10 22	10 32	10 42	10 52	11 2	11 17	11 27	9 12	9 42	9 57	10 12	10 27	10 42	11 12	11 27	11 42		10 12	10 27	10 42	11 2	11 17
Holly Bush	10 14	10 24	10 34	10 44	10 54	11 4	11 19	11 29	9 14	9 44	9 59	10 14	10 29	10 44	11 14	11 29	11 44		10 14	10 29	10 44	11 4	11 19
Tongwynlais	10 17	10 27	10 37	10 47	10 57	11 7	11 22	11 32	9 17	9 47	10 2	10 17	10 32	10 47	11 17	11 32	11 47		10 17	10 32	10 47	11 7	11 22
Taffs Well P.O.	10 21	10 31	10 41	10 51	11 1	11 11	11 26	11 36	9 21	9 51	10 6	10 21	10 36	10 51	11 21	11 36	11 51		10 21	10 36	10 51	11 11	11 26
Nantgarw	10 26	10 36	10 46	10 56	11 6	11 16	11 31	11 41	9 26	9 56	10 11	10 26	10 41	10 56	11 26	11 41	11 56		10 26	10 41	10 56	11 16	11 31
Upper Boat	10 30	10 40	10 50	11 0	11 10	11 20	11 35	11 45	9 30	10 0	10 15	10 30	10 45	11 0	11 30	11 45	12 0		10 30	10 45	11 0	11 20	11 35
Rhydyfelin Station	10 36	10 46	10 56	11 6	11 16	11 26	11 41	11 51	9 36	10 6	10 21	10 36	10 51	11 6	11 36	11 51	12 6		10 36	10 51	11 6	11 26	11 41
Glyntaff	10 38	10 48	10 58	11 8	11 18	11 28	11 43	12 53	9 38	10 8	10 23	10 38	10 53	11 8	11 38	11 53	12 8		10 38	10 53	11 8	11 28	11 43
PONTYPRIDD (Station Square)	—	10 53	11 3	11 13	11 23	11 33		12 58	—	10 13	10 28	—	10 58	11 13	—	11 58	12 13		—	10 58	11 13	11 33	11 48
do. (Queen's Hotel)	10 45	..	..	—	..	..	11 50	..	9 45	..	..	10 45	..	..	11 45	..	..		10 45	..	—	..	—

By 1934 Rhondda Tramways had replaced their railed vehicles with motor-buses, although fourteen years before they had commenced motor operation Pontypridd-Cardiff. This timetable shows a rather rare example of sensible co-operation but as it measures 15" x 12" (38 cm x 30.5 cm) only a part can be reproduced. This is, however, a fine example of a clear, comprehensive document. White's Motors were to sell out to Western Welsh in 1936.

PREMIER LINE LTD.

NEW SERVICE OF STAGE CARRIAGES

Commencing Monday, May 22nd, 1933,

BETWEEN

Slough & Manor Park Estate

(William Street) (Junction of Granville Ave. & Hatton Ave.)

via William Street, Stoke Road, Elliman's Avenue, Stoke Poges Lane, Granville Avenue — Granville Avenue, Stoke Poges Lane, Bath Road, William St.

TIME TABLE—Monday to Friday.

Slough ... (William Street)	10 30	11 15	12 0	12 45	1 30	2 0	2 30	3 0	3 30	5 0	5 30	6 0	6 30
Manor Park Estate (Hatton Avenue)	10 40	11 25	12 10	12 55	1 40	2 10	2 40	3 10	3 40	5 10	5 40	6 19	6 40

Slough ... William Street	7 0	7 30	8 0	8 30	9 0	9 30	10 0	10 30
Manor Park Estate (Hatton Avenue)	7 10	7 40	8 10	8 40	9 10	9 40	10 10	10 40

Manor Park Estate Hatton Avenue)	10 50	11 40	12 20	1 10	1 45	2 15	2 45	3 15	3 45	5 15	5 45	6 15	6 45
Slough ... (William Street)	11 0	11 50	12 30	1 20	1 55	2 25	2 55	3 25	3 55	5 25	5 55	6 25	6 55

Manor Park Estate (Hatton Avenue)	7 15	7 45	8 15	8 45	9 15	9 45	10 15	10 45
Slough ... (William Street)	7 25	7 55	8 25	8 55	9 25	9 55	10 25	10 55

SATURDAYS.

Slough ... (William Street)	10 20	11 0	11 30	12 15	12 45	1 30	Then every **0** & **30** mins past each hour to **10.30**
Manor Park Estate (Hatton Avenue	10 30	11 10	11 40	12 25	12 55	1 40	,, ,, **10 & 40** ,, ,, ,, ,, **10.40**
Manor Park Estate (Hatton Avenue)	10 40	11 15	11 50	12 30	1 15	1 45	Then every **15 & 45** mins. past each hr. to **10.45**
Slough ... (William Street)	10 50	11 25	12 0	12 40	1 25	1 55	, ,, **25 & 55** ,, ,, ,, ,, **10.55**

Restrictions placed on the Service.

A passenger shall not on the same journey both be picked up and set down on that part of the route which lies between the second proposed street west of junction of Granville Avenue and Stoke Poges Lane, and William Street (South end) both places inclusive.

BLACK & WHITE MOTORWAYS, LTD.

Page 63. The following do not make connections on the midnight Ex London Service.

ABERGAVENNY — NANTYMOEL
BLAENGARW — PORTHCAWL
BARGOED — PONTYPRIDD
BLACKWOOD — PENARTH
EBBW VALE — PONTYPOOL
GWAUN CAE GURWEN

No connections through to Valley Towns South Wales Area are made on Sundays in connection with the 12 midnight service departing London.

ookings from

JTH WALES AREA.

					tures ondon p.m.	Mid-night	Change at	Connecting Bus Service
ABERGAVENNY ..	15/–	24/6	8.30	10.30	—	+12.0	Newport	Western Welsh O'bus Co.
AMMANFORD ..	19/3	31/3	8.30	10.30	—	12.0	Neath	,, ,, ,,
BLAENGARW ..	16/9	27/6	8.30	10.30	—	+12.0	Bridgend	,, ,, ,,
BARRY	15/3	24/6	8.30	10.30	—	+12.0	Cardiff	,, ,, ,,
BARGOED ..	15/3	24/6	8.30	10.30	—	+12.0	Newport	,, ,, ,,
BANWEN	18/6	30/–	8.30	10.30	—	+12.0	Neath	South Wales Transport Co.
BLACKWOOD ..	14/6	23/6	8.30	10.30	—	12.0	Newport	Western Valley Motor Ser.
BLAENAVON ..	14/9	23/6	8.30	10.30	—	+12.0	Newport	Eastern Valley Motor Ser.
CROSSKEYS ..	14/–	23/–	8.30	10.30	—	+12.0	Newport	Western Valley Motor Ser.
CARMARTHEN ..	21/3	34/–	8.30	*10.30	—	+12.0	Neath	Western Welsh O'bus Co.
CARDIGAN ..	24/6	38/6	—	—	—	+12.0	Neath	,, ,, ,,
CAERPHILLY ..	14/6	23/6	8.30	10.30	—	+12.0	Newport	,, ,, ,,
EBBW VALE ..	15/6	24/–	8.30	10.30	—	+12.0	Newport	Western Valley Motor Ser.
FISHGUARD ..	26/3	41/–	—	—	—	+12.0	Neath	Western Welsh O'bus Co.
GWAUN CAE GURWEN	19/–	31/–	8.30	—	—	12.0	Swansea	South Wales Transport Co.
GORSEINON ..	18/3	29/6	8.30	10.30	—	+12.0	Swansea	,, ,, ,,
GROESFFORDD ..	22/6	36/6	—	—	—	+12.0	Neath	Western Welsh O'bus Co.
GLYNNEATH ..	18/6	29/6	8.30	—	—	+12.0	Neath	,, ,, ,,
GARNDIFFAITH ..	14/6	23/6	8.30	10.30	—	+12.0	Newport	Eastern Valley Motor Ser.
HIRWAUN.. ..	18/9	30/6	8.30	—	—	+12.0	Neath	Western Welsh O'bus Co.
HAVERFORDWEST	24/6	39/9	—	—	—	+12.0	Neath	,, ,, ,,
LLANDYSSUL ..	23/–	36/9	—	—	—	+12.0	Neath	,, ,, ,,
LLANELLY ..	18/9	30/6	8.30	10.30	—	12.0	Swansea	South Wales Transport Co.
LLANDILO.. ..	20/–	32/–	—	—	—	12.0	Swansea	,, ,, ,,
MAESTEG	16/6	27/9	8.30	10.30	—	+12.0	Bridgend	Western Welsh O'bus Co.
NEW QUAY ..	24/9	39/–	—	—	—	+12.0	Neath	,, ,, ,,
NEWCASTLE EMLYN	23/3	27/3	—	—	—	+12.0	Neath	,, ,, ,,
NARBERTH ..	23/6	38/–	—	—	—	+12.0	Neath	,, ,, ,,
NANTYMOEL ..	16/9	27/6	8.30	10.30	—	+12.0	Bridgend	,, ,, ,,
PORTHCAWL ..	16/6	27/3	8.30	10.30	—	+12.0	Bridgend	,, ,, ,,
PONTYPRIDD ..	15/3	24/6	8.30	10.30	—	+12.0	Cardiff	,, ,, ,,
PENARTH ..	14/6	24/–	8.30	10.30	—	12.0	Cardiff	,, ,, ,,
PONTARDAWE ..	18/6	30/–	*8.30	—	—	12.0	Swansea	South Wales Transport Co.
PONTYBEREM ..	22/9	36/6	—	—	—	+12.0	Neath	Western Welsh O'bus Co.
PONTYPOOL ..	14/–	23/–	8.30	10.30	—	+12.0	Newport	,, ,, ,,
RISCA	13/9	22/6	8.30	10.30	—	+12.0	Newport	Western Valley Motor Ser.
ST. DAVIDS ..	29/9	43/6	—	—	—	+12.0	Neath	Western Welsh O'bus Co.
ST. CLEARS ..	22/3	35/9	—	—	—	+12.0	Neath	,, ,, ,,
TREDEGAR ..	15/–	24/–	8.30	10.30	—	—	Newport	,, ,, ,,
WHITLAND ..	22/9	36/9	—	—	—	+12.0	Neath	,, ,, ,,
YSTRADMYNACH	15/–	24/3	8.30	10.30	—	+12.0	Newport	,, ,, ,,
YSTRADGYNLAIS	19/6	30/9	*8.30	—	—	12.0	Swansea	South Wales Transport Co.
YSTALYFERA ..	19/3	30/6	*8.30	—	—	—	Swansea	,, ,, ,,

*—Not Sundays. +—No connection on Sunday mornings at Transfer Town.

ALL INTERMEDIATE AND ARRIVAL TIMES SHOWN ARE APPROXIMATE ONLY.

▲

Even in the 1930s, probably due to declining traffic as the slump reduced the spare cash in people's pockets (even white collar workers, the 'natural' coach passengers were being affected) timetable alterations became necessary, giving a very unprofessional result. This is drawn from London Coastal Coaches winter booklet 1932/3 when already the Newcastle service showed "lost" independents with "late Glenton Friars Service" and "late National Coachways Service" being replaced by United.

In the 1930s we had the great age of suburban estates with "Metroland" the best known of this new style of housing. The contrast between these "New Towns" and "Garden Cities" with today's newly built miserable breeze-block and plywood "dwellings" is perhaps indicative of the falling standards we find in the country, echoed to some extent by the "converted bread vans" that seem to serve modern estates. This timetable bears not only the service details, but the fares (all the way 2d., Elliman's Avenue to the Estate 1d.) The sheet also draws attention to a restriction, inserted to protect the main local operator.

LLANDUDNO—*continued.*

HENNINGS COACHES
(Henning Bros.)

From **LONDON** a.m. — **Fares** From London
(28, Caledonian Road) 8.30
From **LLANDUDNO** .. a.m. — Sgl. 17/6, Rtn. 30/-
(Rock Drive) 8.30
p.m.
Dep. Shrewsbury (Roland Garage) 1.0 — Sgl. 14/-, Rtn. 26/-
via **Dunstable, Coventry, Birmingham, Stafford.**

LOWESTOFT—*see Yarmouth.*

LUDLOW

BLACK & WHITE MOTORWAYS, LTD.

From **LONDON** (8¾ hrs.) a.m.
(15a, Hammersmith Bdge. Rd., W.6) 11.0
From **LUDLOW** a.m.
(Bull Ring) 10.30
Fares: Sgl. 13/-, Rtn. 21/-
via **Gloucester, Tewkesbury, Worcester.**

LUTON

STRAWHATTER MOTOR COACHES

	a.m.	a.m.	p.m.	p.m.	p.m.	p.m.	p.m.	p.m.
From **LONDON** (Central Station, Cartright Gdns., W.C.1)	8.50	10.40	12.20	1.50	5.20	7.20	9.5	11.30

Sun., 10.40 a.m. and 1.50, 4.20, 7.30 and 10.50 p.m.

	a.m.	a.m.	a.m.	p.m.	p.m.	p.m.	p.m.	p.m.
From **LUTON** (Luton Park Sq.)	7.30	9.0	10.30	12.30	2.0	5.0	7.30	9.30

Sun., 9.0 a.m. and 12.30, 2.0, 6.0 and 9.30 p.m.
via **Tally Ho Corner.**

Fares: Sgl. 2/-, Day Rtn. 2/6, Per. Rtn. 3/-, Children 2/-

IMPERIAL MOTOR SERVICES

Frequent daily service from 4, York Road, King's X, and from Manchester Square, Luton
via **St. Albans.**
Fares: Sgl. 2/-, Day Rtn. 2/6, Per. Rtn. 3/6

MANCHESTER

ENIWAY MOTOR TOURS
(For Intermediate Fares, etc., see page 64)

	a.m.	a.m.	p.m.
From **LONDON** (9½ hrs.) (Central Station, Cartwright Gdns., W.C.1)	9.0	10.0	11.0
From **MANCHESTER** (81a, Peter St.)	9.0	10.30	11.0

Fares: Sgl. 16/6, Rtn. 30/-, Children 1/- over half fare.
via **St. Albans, Dunstable, Towcester, Coventry, Birmingham, Wolverhampton, Stafford, Newcastle-under-Lyme.**

"What should they know of England, Who only tunnels know?"
(With apologies to Mr. Kipling)

TOGNARELLI'S PULLMAN COMFORT COACHES
(J. R. Tognarelli & Co.)

From **LONDON** (9½ hrs.) a.m.
(Central Station, Cartwright Gardens, W.C.1) 9.30
From **MANCHESTER** a.m.
(Opposite Victoria Station) 9.15
Fares: Sgl. 16/6, Rtn. 30/-
For Glasgow, see Bolton and Glasgow.

MAJESTIC SALOON COACH SERVICES

	a.m.	p.m.
From **LONDON** (10 hrs.) (Central Station, Cartwright Gdns., W.C.1.)	9.0	11.0
(317 Regent St., W.1)	9.30	11.30
From **MANCHESTER** (Imperial Buildings, 9, Oxford Road)	9.0	11.0

Fares: Sgl. 16/6, Rtn. 30/-
via **Coventry, Birmingham, Wolverhampton, Newcastle-under-Lyme.**

HOLT'S MOTOR COACHES

From **LONDON** (9½ hrs.) a.m.
(Charing X Embankment) .. 8.30
From **MANCHESTER** a.m.
(St. Peter's Square) 9.0
Fares: Sgl. 16/6, Rtn. 30/-
via **St. Albans, Coventry, Birmingham, Wolverhampton.**

PALANQUIN COACH SERVICES

	a.m.*	p.m.
From **LONDON** (10½ hrs.) (Bush House, Aldwych, W.C.1)	9.0	1.30
From **MANCHESTER** (14, Piccadilly)	9.0	2.0

*Not Sun.
Fares: Sgl. 16/6, Rtn. 30/-
via **High Barnet, Bedford, Kettering, Leicester, Derby, Matlock, Buxton, Stockport.**

ALBATROSS SLEEPING CARS
(For Particulars, etc., see page 60)

From **LONDON** (11 hrs.) p.m.
(53, Woburn Pl., W.C.1) 10.0
From **MANCHESTER**
(83, Mosley Street) .. .. Midnight
Fares: Sgl. 22/6, Rtn. 40/-

MARGATE

UNIQUE MOTOR COACH CO.

	a.m.	p.m.	p.m.	p.m.*
From **LONDON** (3½ hrs.) (215, Vauxhall Bdge. Rd.)	9.0	2.30	7.0	8.0
From **MARGATE** (6, Paradise St.)	8.0	2.30	5.0	

* Sunday only.
Fares: Sgl. 5/-, Day Rtn. 6/6, Per. Rtn. 9/-. After May 18: 7/6, 10/-, 14/-
via **Lewisham, Canterbury.**

THANET EXPRESS COACHES

From **LONDON** (322, Vauxhall Bdge. Rd., S.W.1)	a.m. 9.30	p.m. 2.30	p.m. 6.30		
From **MARGATE** (Cecil Square)	a.m. 8.30	a.m. 9.30	p.m. 2.30	p.m. 4.30	p.m. 6.0

Fares: Sgl. 6/-, Day Rtn. 8/6, Per. Rtn. 10/-

PULLMAN MOTOR COACHES

From **LONDON** (3½ hrs. (Opp. Parnell, Vauxhall Bdge. Rd., S.W.1)	p.m. 3.0	p.m. 7.0
From **MARGATE** (Clock Tower)	a.m. 9.15	p.m. 2.15

Fares: Sgl. 5/6, Rtn. 9/6
via **Canterbury.**

The names of pre-war coach operating companies are a part of the fascination of timetables; Lavender Blue, Orange, Blue Band, Black & White, Redcar (although that's cheating!) and Royal Blue rivalled Morning Star, Victory, Highways, Queen, Eclipse, Fairway, All-weather, Super and a myriad of other concerns, more redolent of the great days of stage coaches than of motor vehicles.

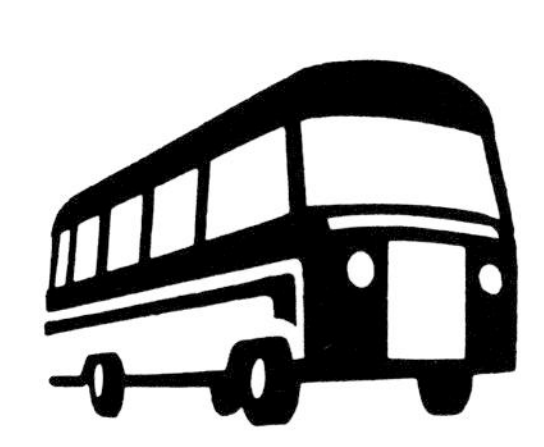

But, Sir or Madam, may we add a timely note from Mr Joseph Roscoe's excellent "Express Motor Coach Service between Preston, Bolton, MANCHESTER,* Birmingham and LONDON*" dated 14 August 1931.

IMPORTANT:- *The attention of passengers is drawn to the importance of re-joining the coach promptly after meals, as unpunctuality leads to serious inconvenience to other passengers having connections to catch at the terminus. Drivers have instructions not to await beyond the allotted time and the Company will not be responsible for passengers left behind in these circumstances.*

DEAR SIR

With the advent of computors and a realisation that bus passengers are numerically in decline, most large operators and many County Councils have made timetables far more accessible. It is true that one can still fax a company enquiring the frequency of a given route and receive no reply; it is also true that if you turn up at the Post Office at Puissant D'Arcy expecting the one-a-day bus to be a blue one belonging to Brown's Cream Buses you may well be disappointed as they have probably just lost the contract - or at least the subsidy - to run this journey to the maroon and white buses of Bedlington Blue Bus Company. But if the council information office has told you a bus will run at 9.21 each day in all probability it will arrive. In 1947 there were four timetabled buses a day but by 1970 matters had reached such a pass that Mrs. Marsh the Postmistress would emerge from the Post Office, ascertain you were going to the town, and telephone 'Arry to tell him he had to run as he had a passenger. You would be late but had you not been a stranger you would, of course, have known to ring 'Arry the night before to confirm your intention to travel. In our case 'Arry would ring me as the nearest operator, we would collect a hire fee, solemnly handing over any fares collected and he would stand the loss, reckoning it cheaper than paying his driver and running a bus every day.

Just after the war travel really was difficult as vehicles were either tired out or desperately uncomfortable (wooden seats were still around in the early 1950s) petrol, the normal fuel of village owner-operators, rationed and many men who had been running buses since 1920 were anxious to retire but had (too often, alas) lost relatives in the Second World War, or the heir apparent had gained a taste for travel while in the Armed Services or acquired a city-born wife who (as many did and do) loathed the countryside. It is claimed that 30% of wartime child evacuees sent from the city to the country had never seen a cow and it gave one a sense of deja-vu to read in the Daily Mail, 21 April 1994, that, writing of inner-city children the correspondent could state: "At this point I realised we had a problem. What was the point of arguing with them, or of my wife trying to teach the children a lesson, when neither the children nor their mother had any concept that they had done anything wrong? They merely thought it was better to take flowers from a private garden than from a public park". Unfortunately for not a few operators the coming of such children whether in 1940 or 1990 can spell the end. What can you say when after remonstrating with a youth for urinating on the *inside* of the coach he tells you, quite unashamedly that you ought to supply a toilet?

So it was really small wonder that in the first few years after the war, if you wanted to travel you enquired what service there was, as in all probability no public timetables had been issued since 1940 and certainly no fixed bus stops existed. Everyone who needed to know knew you waited at 9.20 outside the Blacksmith's Arms, or the Village Hall, or Gibbet Crossroads.

Incredibly some letters from operators have survived the 40-odd years since they were written and give us some confirmation of the problems of the time. For reasons of space only a handful of this type of letter can be reproduced, but enough, I hope, to give the flavour of real country bus work.

PHONE 250

Giant, Car and Tractor Tyres always in Stock

Registered Service Dealers for Giant and Car Tyres

THOMAS JOHNSTON & SON
AUTOMOBILE ENGINEERS
JOHNSTON'S TYRE DEPOT
DALBEATTIE

JMcL/IH

15th December, 1950.

Dear Sir,

Prior to the 1939-45 war, we did run Service between Colvend and Castle Douglas, but this Service was terminated by us due to economic conditions. We have pleasure how: :ever, in detailing below Time Tables of the existing Ser: :vices which we hope you will find suitable.

We assure you of our best attention at all times.

Yours faithfully,
pro: THOMAS JOHNSTON AND SON.
JMcLaughlin

Weekdays Only (Winter)

Penmans Service - (Sandyhills, Colvend & Dalbeattie)

Leave Sandyhills	- 9.30am	12.30pm	4.30pm
Arrive Dalbeattie	-10 AM	1.00pm	5.00pm
Leave Dalbeattie	- 8.45am	11.45am	3.45pm
Arrive Sandyhills	_ 9.15am	12.15am	4.15pm

Western S.M.T. Service (Kippford, Dalbeattie & Castle Douglas

Leave Kippford	9.45am	11.55am	5.50pm
Arrive Dalbeattie	10am	12.10pm	6.05pm
Leave Dalbeattie	10am	12.15pm	6.20pm
Arrive Castle-Douglas	10.25am	12.40pm	6.45pm
Leave Castle-Douglas	11.10am	5.10pm	
Arrive Dalbeattie	11.35am	5.35pm	
Arrive Kippford	11.55am	5.50pm	

SEAS... EXCURSIONS ARE CHEAPER MID-WEEK

SPORTS AND SUPPORTERS' CLUBS BY SEASON & SPECIAL FIXTURES

THEATRES AND DANCE PARTIES TRAVEL TOGETHER IN COMFORT

"YOUR PLEASURE IS OUR BUSINESS."

DODDS' Telephone Numbers 97-487

LUXURY COACHES

DODDS' (COACHES) LTD.,

Office: 72 PORTLAND STREET, TROON.

15th January, 1951.

Dear Sir,

In reply to your letter of 13th inst.

1. Troon (Portland Garage) & Troon (Harbour) - This Service has been discontinued as the Pleasure Steamer does not now call at Troon Harbour. Persons wishing to take advantage of these Clyde sailings have to join the Steamer at Ayr Harbour.
2. Troon - Dumfries - This service has been discontinued since the war but we intend starting it again this season. This particular service, of course, is part of an inclusive tour costing £ 12.12.0 for eight days (Saturday to Saturday) starting and finishing at Dumfries but only available to people travelling from Stations South of Dumfries.

We have not, as yet, completed arrangements with the Hotels regarding accommodation, but, as soon as this is arranged, printed material will be available describing the Tour in full.

Thanking you for this enquiry,

We remain,

WD/DW. Yours faithfully,

THE JOURNEY IS PART OF THE OUTING - TRAVEL BY ROAD

Phone: 89 BYFLEET.

HOWARD'S GARAGE

PROPRIETOR: HARRY HOWARD, (A.M.I.B.E.)

WEST BYFLEET, SURREY

MOTOR ENGINEERS AND REPAIRERS

Singer and Austin Agents
Hire Service of Taxis, Coaches and Private Cars

February "28th.1958.

Dear Sir,

In answer to your letter dated 25th, February re Stage service.

The only Stage Service we run is on Sunday afternoons between W.Byfleet Station and Pyrford Hospital.

Yours faithfully,

p/p H Howard
H. Howard

TELEPHONE: TIMBERSCOMBE 242 — ACCESSORIES AND REPAIRS

THE GARAGE, WOOTTON COURTENAY
MINEHEAD

BURNELL'S GARAGE

Props.: I. T. & G. H. BURNELL

Any make of Car or Motor Cycle supplied
Terms and Exchanges

* All vehicles driven and stored at Owners' risk *
REBORING AND VALVE REFACING
Done on the premises on "VAN NORMAN" machines
ALSO OXY-ACETYLENE WELDING & CUTTING

CARS - - COACHES AND LORRIES FOR HIRE

April 5th 1958

Dear Sir,

We have curtailed our Bus Service since last Summer. It now runs Thursday & Saturdary afternoon.

Time Table

Thursdays

Wootton Courtenay depart 10 AM arrive MINEHEAD 10.30 (Via Dunster)
" " " 2 PM " " 2.30

MINEHEAD depart 12 NOON arrive Wootton Courtenay 12.30 PM
" " 4.30 PM " " " 5 PM

Saturday

Depart Wootton Courtenay 2 PM & depart MINEHEAD 5 PM

Yours faithfully
I.T. Burnell

Bailey's Bus Services

COACHES FOR PRIVATE HIRE

HAULAGE CONTRACTORS & COACH PROPRIETORS

FANGFOSS

YORK

Telephone: Bishop Wilton 235

ALL CLASSES OF HAULAGE UNDERTAKEN

COMMENCING
23rd MAY, 1961.

TIME TABLE

POCKLINGTON, FANGFOSS, STAMFORD BRIDGE, WESTOW, MALTON.

MONDAY to FRIDAY

		a m				p m				
POCKLINGTON dep.		7.30		11.0	11.30		1.45	2.30	5.30	9.45
Fangfoss		7.40	9.40	11.10	11.40	1.40	1.55	2.40	5.40	9.55
Stamford Bridge		8.0	10.0	Mon	Tues	2.0		3.0	6.0	
Westow		8.20		Wed	Fri.			3.20		
MALTON arr.		8.45		Thurs.				3.45		
MALTON Newgate				9.15					4.15	
Westow				9.40					4.40	
Stamford Bridge			9.0	10.0	11.0			3.0	5.0	7.0
Fangfoss	7.0	7.15	9.15	10.15	11.15	2.15	3.0	3.15	5.15	7.15
POCKLINGTON arr	7.10	7.25		10.25		2.25	3.10		5.25	

SATURDAYS ONLY

POCKLINGTON dep.		7.30	9.30	11.30		2.30	8.30
Fangfoss		7.40	9.40	11.40	1.40	2.40	8.40
Stamford bridge		8.0	10.0	12.0	2.0	3.0	9.0
Westow		8.20		12.20		3.20	
MALTON arr.		8.45		12.45		3.45	
MALTON Newgate		9.15		1.15		4.15	
Westow		9.40		1.40		4.40	
Stamford Bridge		10.0		2.0		5.0	9.0
Fangfoss	7.15	10.15	9.0	2.15		5.15	9.15
POCKLINGTIN	7.25	10.25	9.10	2.25		5.25	

SUNDAYS ONLY

POCKLINGTON			3.45		7.30	9.45
Fangfoss	9.40		4.0		7.40	9.55
Stamford Bridge	10.0				8.0	
Stamford Bridge	11.0		3.0			9.0
Fangfoss		1.0		5.0	7.0	9.15
POCKLINGTON arr.		1.10		5.10	7.10	9.25

FARE STAGES

Yapham Mill, Smylett Corner, Bolton, Fangfoss, Gowthorpe Lane, Full Sutton, Full Sutton Bkyds., Stamford Bridge, Burtonfields, Skirpenbeck Lane, Buttercrambe Bridge, Scrayingham Gate, Leppington Lane, Gally Gap, Westow, Firby Lane, Huttons Ambo Lane, Norton Crossing, MALTON (Newgate).

JOHN MacCUISH

CIVIL ENGINEERING and HAULAGE CONTRACTOR

MALAGLATE, SOLLAS, NORTH UIST

TELEPHONE SOLLAS 211

8th Sept. 1973

Dear Sir,

I am in receipt of your letter requesting a copy of the current timetable for my bus service. As you are aware this is operated for school children travelling to Paible J.S. School. The details are as follows:-

Mon. to Fri. (during school session)

7.45 am Bus departs from Sollas to Lochmaddy.

8.10 am Bus departs from Lochmaddy, travelling via Sollas & collecting children en route.

9.10 am Bus arrived as Paible J.S. School. After children have alighted bus travels back to Sollas.

3.30 pm Bus leaves Sollas for Paible J.S. School.

4.05 pm Bus leaves Paible J.S. School & travels to Lochmaddy via Sollas & then back to Sollas again.

I trust that this information will be of use to you. May I mention that Mr. J. Garbutt, Benbecula, South Uist also operates a School Bus Service.

Yours faithfully
J. MacCuish

MacDonald Arms Hotel

TOBERMORY

Isle of Mull

ALEXANDER COWE
PROPRIETOR

PHONE 11

CARS FOR HIRE

Date *15th April 1966*

Dear Sir,

My husband who usually attends to letters has had a stroke and on going through letters I find one from you regarding bus services. We have now sold our bus services to David MacBrayne so if you contact them they will give you the information. I must apologise for any inconvenience caused.

Yours faithfully
E.N. Cowe

TRANSPORT HARDSHIP IN RURAL AREAS.

Ruthless cuts in long-distance coach and country bus services have been necessitated by the urgent need for economy in petrol and rubber consumption. Regional Transport Commissioners, always presented with cogent reasons why this or that service should be retained, are doing their best to ensure that undue hardship is not being felt in any district.

At the same time, the number of complaints coming from rural districts shows that workers and housewives in isolated places are suffering real hardships in their efforts to make necessary journeys.

Surely something can be done to mitigate the hardships. When a rural bus service is withdrawn, a shuttle service to the nearest main road or station might be substituted. Where train services between towns are unsuitably timed, or fares are more expensive than the coach services, these need not be cut out completely, but rather a reduced number of coaches might be allowed to run at a time of day when a train is not available. To effect a saving to counterbalance this, coaches could discharge their passengers at the town's limits, whence the journey could be completed on the local buses or trams.

In certain regions such ideas are already being put into practice. The well-being and efficiency of a number of country dwellers depends on their extension.

Country location for a bucolic crowd.
Smiths of Reading Panorama bodied coaches.
Sometime in the early 1970s.

REVISED SERVICE

During the year that these photographs were taken, 1992, the village of Rowney Green near Alvechurch, Worcestershire, was served by one bus a week as had been the case for many years. It is, of course, a commutor dormitory, losing all its three shops in the late 1970s, and its public telephone shortly afterwards. About ten years ago the Women's Institute died and the Playing fields were (to all intents and purposes) handed over to 'foreign' football teams. Most inhabitants have one car plus an 'All-Terrain' Range Rover-type vehicle plus horse, etc. But there are just a handful of, mainly elderly, people who cannot, do not or would not want to drive. The one bus runs on Fridays and allows about 3 hours shopping time in the local market town of Redditch, but in 1992 both Christmas Day and New Year's Day fell on a Friday, so this unusual Thursday working was recorded by a photographer.

Notice at the local village hall.

C385 RUY, Mercedes-Benz L608D with 1986 built Robin Hood 20 seat bodywork, No. 1385 in the fleet of Midland Red West (now part of Badgerline) loads on a dank depressing day.

And departs past the old Post Office to Redditch at 0944.

— Travelling Buses —

In more ways than are at first apparent it is fitting that the last photograph in this book should be of a genuine 1947 'home-built' B.M.M.O. (Midland Red) S6, No. 3098 leaving Market Square, Warwick on Saturday, 20 July 1963.

Goodbye, Midland Red

— Index —

– BODY & CHASSIS MANUFACTURERS' INDEX –